Library of
Davidson College

Inequity and Intervention

The Federal Budget and Central America

**PACCA SERIES ON THE DOMESTIC ROOTS OF
U.S. FOREIGN POLICY**

Inequity and Intervention:
The Federal Budget and Central America

Joshua Cohen and Joel Rogers

South End Press   **Boston, MA**

Copyright © 1986 by Joshua Cohen and Joel Rogers

Copyrights are still required for book production in the United States. However, in our case it is a disliked necessity. Thus, any properly footnoted quotation of up to 500 sequential words may be used without permission, as long as the total number of words quoted does not exceed 2000. For longer quotations or for a greater volume of words quoted, written permission from the publisher is required.

First edition
Editing, typesetting, layout by South End Press, Boston
Manufactured in the USA

Library of Congress Cataloguing in Publication Data
Cohen, Joshua 1951-
Inequity and intervention
Budget—United States. 2. United States—Foreign relations —Central America. 3. Central America—Foreign relations—United States. I Rogers, Joel 1952- II Title.
HJ2051.C57   1986   337.91'73'0728   86-3755
ISBN 0-89608-325-X

SOUTH END PRESS   116 St. Botolph St.   BOSTON, MA 02115

Domestic Roots Statement

Domestic Roots of U.S. Foreign Policy is a project of Policy Alternatives for the Caribbean and Central America (PACCA), an association of scholars and policymakers. Through research, analysis, policy recommendations, and the collaboration of analysts in the U.S. and the Caribbean Basin, PACCA aims to promote a humane and democratic alternative to present U.S. policies toward Central America and the Caribbean.

The principles of such an alternative are set forth in PACCA's *Changing Course: Blueprint for Peace in Central America and the Caribbean*:

> U.S. foreign policy should be based on the principles which it seeks to further in the world. These include: non-intervention, respect for self-determination, collective self-defense, peaceful settlement of disputes, respect for human rights, support for democratic development and concern for democratic values. Adherence to these principles is critical to working out practical programs for regional peace and development.

Participants in the *Domestic Roots* project endorse these principles, and seek to widen discussion of alternative policies based on them. The project explores the links between current U.S. policies in the region and major institutions and issues in U.S. domestic politics. In a series of pamphlets, *Domestic Roots* will highlight the continuity between domestic policy initiatives and current policies in the region, locate the domestic sources of current policy choices there, and assess the obstacles to and opportunities for widening debate about those policies, and constructing a decent and democratic alternative to them.

PACCA Executive Board

Robert Armstrong, North American Congress on Latin America
Roger Burbach, Center for Study of the Americas
Joseph Collins, Institute for Food and Development Policy
Michael Conroy, University of Texas
Carmen Diana Deere, University of Massachusetts
Richard R. Fagen, Stanford University
Xabier Gorostiaga, Regional Office for Economic and Social Research, Managua
Saul Landau, Institute for Policy Studies
William LeoGrande, American University

Domestic Roots Project

Robert Armstrong, North American Congress on Latin America; PACCA Executive Board
Joshua Cohen, Masachusetts Institute of Technology
Frances Fox Piven, City University of New York
Joel Rogers, Rutgers University
Juliet Schor, Harvard University; Center for Popular Economics
Mark Tushnet, Georgetown University Law Center

PACCA Executive Director: Robert Stark
PACCA Outreach Staff: Joy Hackel

A nation that continues year after year to spend more money on military defense than on programs of social uplift is approaching spiritual death.
—Martin Luther King, Jr., 1967

Table of Contents

Acknowledgements	xi
Introduction	1
1 Historical Background	5
1 Spending: Guns and Butter	5
1.1 Military	5
1.2 Social Spending	11
2 Taxes: Passing the Bucks	14
2 The Reagan Budget	19
1 Outlays: The Days of Spend and Spend	21
1.1 Social Spending	22
1.2 Military	24
1.3 Interest on the Debt	30
2 Tax Cuts: Feeding the Hogs	33
3 The Bottom Line: Inequality and the Politics of Deficts	35
3 Central America: A Budgetary Perspective	39
1 The Policy Framework: Low Intensity Warfare/High Intensity Symbolism	39
2 U.S. Policy in Central America: "No Free Lunch"	42
2.1 "Security" Assistance	42
2.2 Maintaining Presence	45
2.3 No Force Without Forces	46
2.4 Balance Sheets	48
3 What Next? The Costs of Invasion	49
4 Broadening the Debate: The Costs of Intervention	51
4 Conclusion: Drawing the Line in Central Ameica	53
Footnotes	57
Resources	63

Tables

Table 1:	Military Spending as a Percentage of GNP	6
Table 2:	Income Security Programs, 1950-1980	13
Table 3:	Effective Tax Rates by Population Group, 1966 and 1980	15
Table 4:	Spending Reductions in 1985 as a Result of 1981-84 Policy Changes	23
Table 5:	Ownership of Financial Assets, 1983	31
Table 6:	Estimated Changes in 1984 Tax Bills as a Result of 1981 Tax Cuts, Inflation and Increased Social Security Taxes	34

Figures

Figure 1:	Real Military Spending, 1946-1980 (1986 Dollars)	7
Figure 2:	The Increasing Role of Payroll Taxes	16
Figure 3:	Real Military Spending, 1955-1985 (1972 Dollars)	25
Figure 4:	The Weapons-Driven Buildup	27

Boxes

Box 1:	Regressive Taxes	14
Box 2:	Payroll Taxes	17
Box 3:	Gramm-Rudman and Deficit Reduction	32
Box 4:	Central America: The Basics	40
Box 5:	What's Behind the Mules?	47
Box 6:	Never Say "Never"	50

ACKNOWLEDGEMENTS

We would like to thank the following people for their valuable advice and assistance in writing this essay: Michael Albert, Robert Armstrong, Deborah Barry, Beth Benton, Sam Bowles, David Brooks, Roger Burbach, Betsy Cohn, Gerald Epstein, Joshua Epstein, Jeanne Gallo, Steve Gary, Eva Gold, Richard Healey, Tad Homer-Dixon, William Kaufmann, Michael Klare, Mieke Meurs, Thomas Michl, Vivian Morris, Clare Pastore, Cynthia Peters, Francis Fox Piven, Earl Ravenal, Gretchen Ritter, Katherine Sciacchitano, Juliet Schor, David Slaney, Robert Stark, Charles Stewart, Kip Tiernan, Lupe Tovares, and Mark Tushnet. Special thanks to Joy Hackel for advice, assistance, and suggestions, and for preparing the list of resources at the end of the pamphlet.

Cambridge, MA and New York City　　　　　　　　J.C. and J.R.
January 15, 1986

Introduction

Over the past five years the Reagan administration has made sweeping changes in U.S. domestic policy. Through legislation, it has secured substantial cuts in social spending, and implemented a major regressive shift in the federal tax system. Through executive action, it has dismantled a host of regulatory programs, scaled back government protection of civil rights and civil liberties, and pursued a relentless assault on an already weakened labor movement. By vastly increasing the size of federal deficits, the Administration has also created enormous long term pressures to narrow the range of domestic government activity.

Abroad, these domestic initiatives have been complemented by an exceptionally aggressive foreign policy. The Administration has sponsored the largest sustained peacetime military buildup in U.S. history. It has sabotaged all efforts at arms control with the Soviet Union. And it has demonstrated a renewed U.S. willingness to intervene in the affairs of other states, particularly in the Third World.

Central America and the Caribbean have provided a special focus for the Administration's foreign policy efforts. Aggressive actions in that region began almost the day Reagan took office, with the suspension of U.S. aid to the government of Nicaragua. They have escalated from there. The Administration has promoted the militarization of Honduras, supported and funded the violence of the government of El Salvador, invaded Grenada, pursued a program of nearly constant military exercises in the region, and mounted a broad campaign of war and destabilization against the government of Nicaragua.

While they are often analyzed in isolation from one another, we believe the Reagan domestic and foreign policy initiatives are related. In this pamphlet we explore those relations, with special reference to Reagan administration policies in Central America. We focus our analysis on the U.S. budget, because the full spectrum of Reagan administration policies are crystallized in the shifting budgetary commitments of the past five years.

The pamphlet has four parts:

Part 1 provides a brief historical overview of the evolution of federal spending and tax policy, concentrating on the period from the end of World War II to the end of the 1970s. The overview highlights that: (1) large peacetime military spending is a recent phenomenon in the U.S., dating from the mid-1950s; (2) peacetime military spending remained relatively constant (correcting for inflation) between 1955 and 1980; (3) the bulk of social spending increases since the mid-1960s is accounted for by the major "social insurance" programs (Social Security and Medicare); and (4) since the mid-1960s, the federal tax burden has shifted away from corporations and wealthier Americans and toward poor and middle income citizens.

Part 2 examines the major changes in the budget during the Reagan period. These changes include: (1) a massive "weapons-driven" military buildup; (2) significant cuts in low income programs; and (3) increased tax burdens for those near the bottom of the income scale and sharply decreased burdens for those near the top. In this section, we also consider some of the consequences of those policies, emphasizing (4) the increasing levels of inequality in the United States, and (5) the ways that the Reagan deficits limit future political choices.

Part 3 places the Reagan Central America policy in this budgetary context. The major points here are that: (1) Central America is a high-intensity symbol and a major testing ground for a broader interventionist foreign policy; (2) current policies in the region now cost nearly $10 billion each year, far more than the Administration acknowledges; and (3) the costs of these regional policies are one part of the more than $100 billion spent each year on an interventionist foreign policy.

Part 4 brings together the different strands of the argument. The magnitude of the costs of current U.S. policies in Central America and the Caribbean, and the broader costs of intervention, underscore the tradeoffs in domestic policy required by the pursuit of intervention. Central America, we conclude, is a good place to draw the line against those tradeoffs, and to contest the foreign policy that imposes them.

Before turning to the budget, we want to state three general views that provide the background for our argument.

First, the issues we address here—justice at home and the conduct of foreign policy—are matters of general public concern, and not just the special interests of professional politicians and policy analysts. In writing this pamphlet, we have therefore tried to avoid the technical terminology of policy debate. Where we have found such terminology unavoidable, we have included explanations of it, either in the text or in the many inserts that supplement the main text.

Second, we believe that there is substantial public opposition in the U.S. to both the foreign and domestic policies of the Reagan administration. Notwithstanding the considerable personal popularity of Ronald Reagan, many Americans oppose the domestic initiatives of the Administration, or some part of those initiatives; others oppose its dangerous foreign policy, or some aspect of that policy. But for all the different issues around which opposition has emerged —from farm policy and unemployment to Star Wars and South Africa—there are at least as many divisions among those who resist the present course of U.S. policy. Seldom coordinated, and sometimes working at cross-purposes, the different movements of opposition are less than the sum of their parts.

Just as fragmentation weakens opposition, coordination and alliance building would strengthen it. Addressing ourselves to anyone concerned about social justice, *either at home or abroad*, we wish to point out possible lines of alliance by showing how current U.S. efforts in Central America undermine domestic interests. Our focus on the material costs of intervention highlights just one way in which this happens. In addition to the tremendous pain they inflict on people in the region, U.S. actions in Central America, and the broader interventionist policies of which they are the cutting edge, impose enormous material costs on citizens of the United States.

Third, and finally, we believe that current U.S. policies in Central America are wrong. The fact that we give special attention to the material costs of those policies does not mean that we think that they are wrong *because* of their costs. Even if they cost nothing at all, we would still think they were wrong. Equally, however, we do not think that paying attention to costs and budgets obscures moral issues. Budgets tell more about a society than the quantity of money that it spends on programs. As the British Prime Minister William Gladstone once observed, budgets are "not merely matters of arithmetic." They provide a record of the choices that governments make and of the values to which they direct their energies. Studying the budget of our own government and the choices it has made thus does not distract from moral judgment. To the contrary, by indicating the enormous consequences of budgetary choices it provides a focus for moral judgments, and underscores the need to make them.

1 Historical Background

In assessing the significance of the policy choices and budgetary tradeoffs now being made in Washington, it helps to have some historical perspective on government spending and taxes. This is where we begin.

1 Spending: Guns and Butter

The government spends money on many things, from soap in the washrooms of federal courthouses to Social Security checks and MX missiles. To get a handle on the large sums involved—$950 billion in 1985—it is useful to look at major *categories* of spending. The broad categories that dominate current budget debate are military and social spending. For that reason, our historical review concentrates on them.

1.1 Military

For the past generation, large peacetime military budgets have been a stable feature of American political life. For all the generations before that, however, they were not. Until the 1950s, the peacetime military share of the Gross National Product (GNP)—the total value of goods and services produced in the U.S.—was relatively modest. Before World War II it averaged about 1 percent per year. (see Table 1).

Table 1: Military Spending as a Percentage of GNP

Year	Federal Spending as a Percentage of GNP	Military Spending as a Percentage of GNP
1905	2.3	1.0
1915	1.9	0.9
1925	3.1	0.8
1935	9.0	1.2
1940	10.0	1.7
1945	42.7	38.2
1955	18.0	11.2
1965	17.9	7.7
1975	22.5	5.8
1985 (est.)	24.8	6.6

Sources: Historical Statistics of the United States, Series F6-9, Y457-465; Historical Tables, Budget of the United States Government, 1986, Table 3.1.

During the war, of course, military spending skyrocketed. Then, after the sharp postwar demobilization between 1945 and 1948, it shot up again by nearly 40 percent in real terms (that is, after inflation) in 1949, and then tripled with the Korean War. When that war ended, however, there was a relatively small 20 percent drop in military spending. As a result, peacetime military outlays levelled off in the late 1950s at more than 12 times their 1940 level. Over the 1955-64 period, they accounted for more than 50 percent of the federal budget and 10 percent of U.S. GNP.[1]

Much more important to the economy than it had been before, military spending also subsidized the development of an enormous armaments industry in the U.S. Remarking on this new development, President Eisenhower observed in his Farewell Address that: "Our military organization today bears little relation to that known by any of my predecessors in peacetime, or indeed by the fighting men of World War II and Korea." Claiming that the U.S. had been "compelled to create a permanent armaments industry of vast proportions," Eisenhower warned that

> [T]he conjunction of an immense Military Establishment and large arms industry is new in the American experience... In the councils of government we must

Historical Background

guard against the acquisition of unwarranted influence whether sought or unsought, by the military-industrial complex. The potential for the disastrous rise of misplaced power exists and will persist.

Once it had reached its new level, however, peacetime military spending remained relatively stable over the 1955-1980 period (see Figure 1), a point worth emphasizing in view of the magnitude of the military buildup since 1980. Between 1955 and 1965, the largest yearly spending increase was just over 4 percent, and that

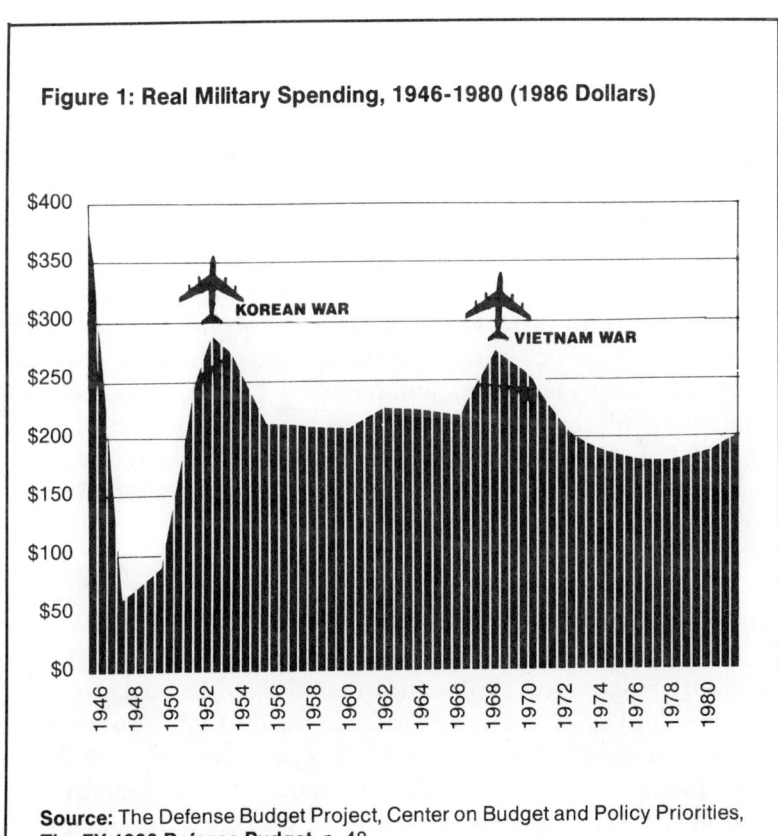

Figure 1: Real Military Spending, 1946-1980 (1986 Dollars)

Source: The Defense Budget Project, Center on Budget and Policy Priorities, **The FY 1986 Defense Budget**, p. 48.

was followed by a 3 percent decrease the following year. The largest four year increase—between 1960 and 1964—was also 4 percent, and that was followed by a 9 percent drop in 1965. The Vietnam War interrupted this steady state. U.S. outlays increased substantially over the 1966-70 period, and after the extensive modernization of U.S. forces during the War, in the early and mid-1970s military spending dropped slightly below its pre-Vietnam levels. But even at their lowest point, in 1976, real military outlays were only 10 percent below the level reached just before the beginning of the Vietnam buildup. And even with the downturn in spending in the mid-70s, the average military share of GNP between 1974 and 1980 was 5.3 percent. The peacetime military budget remained a central element of the American political economy and way of life.[2]

But stability aside, why did the U.S. spend so much on military forces? There are many explanations. Some focus on the "unwarranted influence" of the "military-industrial complex" that Eisenhower warned about, and emphasize the ways that such major military contractors as General Dynamics, General Electric, and Boeing use their political leverage to drive Congress to fund large military outlays. Other accounts center on the economic functions of military spending. They argue that steady infusions of money into the military sector help to keep the economy from stagnating, and permit the government to target and subsidize new technologies and emerging industries.[3] Still other explanations, of course, find the source of high military spending in the "Soviet Threat." They argue that the U.S. has been driven to large peacetime military budgets by the need to defend itself against the Soviet Union.

The military-industrial complex, the different economic functions that military spending performs, and the pattern of U.S.-Soviet relations are all part of the story of the huge U.S. military budget. But explanations relying on these factors alone are incomplete, and can be seriously misleading. The military-industrial complex and economic explanations, for example, do not explain the frequency with which the U.S. has actually *used* military force, as opposed to simply subsidizing its production. A comprehensive study of the U.S. use of military "force without war" in the postwar period found that between 1946 and 1975, even leaving aside the Korean and Vietnam Wars, the United

States used its military forces as an instrument of foreign policy goals 215 times—*once every seven weeks*.[4] An explanation of military spending must also provide an account of what that spending was eventually used for. Given the extensive use of military force by the U.S. in the postwar period, the military-industrial complex and economic-function explanations of military spending fall short.

The problems with the Soviet Threat explanation are more complicated. It is certainly true that the Soviet Union is a repressive society with an enormous military apparatus, and that it competes with the U.S. for influence in the world. Everything else being equal, if the Soviet Union had no military power it seems likely that the U.S. would spend less on military forces. But jumping from these obvious points to the conclusion that U.S. military spending is explained by a more specific *threat* from the Soviet Union seems unjustified for several reasons.

First, the big buildup in U.S. peacetime military spending in the 1950s came at a time when, *on all accounts*, the Soviet Union was significantly weaker as a military power than the U.S. In the years since, the timing of the introduction of major new weapons systems also shows the U.S. consistently leading the Soviet Union. Commenting on nuclear weapons, for example, George Kennan, one-time Ambassador to the Soviet Union, observed:

> [W]e must remember that it has been we Americans who, at almost every step of the road, have taken the lead in the development of this sort of weaponry. It was we who first produced and tested such a device; we who were the first to raise its destructiveness to a new level with the hydrogen bomb; we who introduced the multiple warhead; we who have declined every proposal for the renunciation of the principle of "first use"; and we alone, so help us God, who have used the weapon in anger against others, and tens of thousands of helpless non-combatants at that...[L]et us not, in the face of this record, so lose ourselves in self-righteousness and hypocrisy as to forget the measure of our own complicity in creating the situation we face today.[5]

Moral questions aside, the history that Kennan reviews does not support the claim that the U.S. has only built new weapons in reaction to an external Soviet Threat.

Second, it is revealing that on most of the occasions that the U.S. used military force in the postwar period the Soviet Union was not involved. Leaving aside the 1946-48 period of high U.S.-Soviet tension, for example, the Soviets were involved in only 30 percent of the uses of "force without war" just cited.[6]

Third, while U.S. policy makers have consistently emphasized major new threats from the Soviet Union to justify major new initiatives in U.S. military spending, those threats have just as consistently proven to be non-existent. This was true of the "bomber gap" of the mid-1950s, the "missile gap" used to justify the buildup of U.S. ICBMs in the early 1960s, and both the "window of vulnerability" and the alleged U.S. "unilateral disarmament" of the 1970s used by the Reagan administration to justify the current buildup. Just as consistently, however, the discovery of the non-existence of these "threats" has not brought an end to the buildups they were claimed to justify.[7]

All of this suggests that repeated invocation of the "Soviet Threat" has less to do with assessments of Soviet military might and the danger it poses to the U.S. than with political calculations about how to "sell" increased military spending to a public that might otherwise resist it. Military analysts themselves sometimes acknowledge such calculations. As Samuel Huntington, a prominent Vietnam War hawk and current director of Harvard University's Center for International Affairs, observed in a 1981 roundtable discussion on the lessons U.S. policymakers should draw from the Vietnam War:

> you may have to sell it [intervention or other military action] in such a way as to create the misimpression that it is the Soviet Union that you are fighting. That is what the United States has done ever since the Truman Doctrine.[8]

These problems with conventional explanations suggest the need to look elsewhere in explaining high levels of peacetime military spending in the postwar period. This is not the place to develop an alternative explanation, but the most important part of any account, we believe, must be the distinctive international role the U.S. assumed in the postwar world. The great increase in peacetime military outlays came in the immediate postwar period, when the U.S. emerged as the world's dominant economic and political power. The U.S. consolidated this power in a set of international trade and monetary institutions, and an elaborate framework of military alliance with the leading non-Soviet powers, which together comprised a new international order. The United States was the chief beneficiary and recognized leader of the new system. But this system itself, and the economic and political rewards that the U.S. drew from it, were never without resistance or challenge. The purchase, deployment, and use of vastly expanded military power was essential to playing the leadership role, and a precondition for sustaining U.S. economic and political dominance.

1.2 Social Spending

While military spending was a key element in the postwar budget, the current size and role of the federal budget is not just a result of spending on military forces. Social programs have also expanded significantly in the past 50 years, although the pace and size of that expansion has been very different from the growth of the military.

The growth of social spending programs began with the New Deal. It was then that the federal goverment initiated a system of programs to provide some minimal protection for the income of retired and unemployed Americans, for dependent children, and for those elderly poor who were not eligible for the new program of Social Security. These income maintenance programs, which together comprise the core of the U.S. "welfare state," were gradually supplemented to include public housing and aid for the disabled. But as late as 1960, the basic income security programs together amounted to little more than 3 percent of GNP.[9]

Beginning in the mid-1960s, however, widespread popular pressures converged with elite commitments to fiscal expansion to produce a vast increase in social spending. In the heyday of the Great Society, benefits and coverage provided by existing programs were increased, and a variety of new programs, including Medicare and Medicaid, were added. Further increases came in the late 1960s and early 1970s. Taking just the basic social spending programs whose benefits are paid to individuals, and excluding unemployment insurance (the dimensions of which are particularly sensitive to variations in economic performance), social spending increased dramatically as a share of the budget over the 1960-1975 period. It rose from 16.6 to 31.6 percent of federal outlays and from 3 to 7 percent of GNP.

In characterizing the expansion of social spending, it is important to distinguish between different types of income maintenance programs. Again putting unemployment insurance to the side, they fall broadly into two types. Some—primarily Social Security and Medicare—provide coverage for people in the United States regardless of their income level. These are generally referred to as "social insurance" programs. Others—for example, Food Stamps, Aid to Families with Dependent Children (AFDC), School Lunch and Breakfast programs, and Medicaid—provide benefits only to people with income below a specified level. They are known as "means-tested" programs.[10]

Both sorts of income maintenance programs aim at reducing poverty, or cushioning individuals from the harmful consequences of uncontrolled markets. Social Security, for example, has served as a massive and very successful transfer payment program—transferring monies from those who work to those who are retired—which has lifted millions of elderly Americans out of the ranks of the poor. AFDC, on the other hand, despite much mythology about "welfare cheats" (who, the story goes, never work and never want to), essentially provides short-term income maintenance for those who are temporarily unemployed.

But while the beneficiaries of social programs have much in common, three differences in the structure of the programs from which they benefit tend to divide them in budget politics.

First, as Table 2 indicates, there are considerable differences in the size of programs. Means-tested programs never grew to as much as 10 percent of the federal budget. Social Security and Medicare, on the other hand, increased from 15 to 25 percent of the total budget over the 1965-80 period.

Second, as the difference in size of spending suggests, the basic social insurance programs provide benefits to much larger groups. Virtually *all* people in the U.S. benefit from Social Security or Medicare once they turn 65, and they continue to receive benefits until they die. Much smaller numbers benefit from the means-tested programs, and then for much shorter periods of time.

Third, the means-tested programs are financed out of general government revenues—that is, they are financed by revenues

Table 2: Income Security Programs, 1950-1980

	Social Security, Medicare Spending			Means-tested Income Security Spending		
	Billions of $	% of budget	% of GNP	Billions of $	% of budget	% of GNP
1950	0.8	1.8	0.2	1.7	3.9	0.4
1955	4.4	6.5	1.2	2.4	3.5	0.6
1960	11.6	12.6	2.3	3.7	4.0	0.7
1965	17.5	14.8	2.6	5.4	4.6	0.8
1970	36.5	18.6	3.8	10.4	5.3	1.1
1975	77.5	23.3	5.2	27.5	8.3	1.8
1978	116.6	25.4	5.6	38.6	8.4	1.9
1980	150.6	25.5	5.8	51.7	8.7	2.0

Source: Historical Tables, Tables 1.1, 1.2, 11.3, 13.3.

generated from the personal and corporate income taxes. In this respect, they are just like the military budget, and programs in agriculture, transportation, or education. By contrast, Social Security and most Medicare payments are financed by "payroll" taxes on wage and salary income. The receipts from these taxes are placed in special trust funds, and income from these funds cannot be used to finance other federal programs.

These differences in size, coverage, and financing tend to produce a stronger and better defended constituency for social insurance programs than for means-tested programs. Because the constituency for means-tested programs is smaller, poorer, and less stable, and therefore weaker and less organized, the programs from which they benefit are easier to cut or eliminate than the social insurance programs. As former Office of Management and Budget Director David Stockman once observed about budgetary politics: "Unorganized groups cannot play this game."[11]

2 Taxes: Passing the Bucks

The government's ability to spend depends finally on its power to tax. There are many ways to exercise that power, ranging from taxes on personal or corporate income, to payroll, sales, or property taxes. These different tax "instruments" have importantly different consequences for the distribution of tax payments, that is, for who really bears the tax burden. In assessing the different instruments it is common to classify them according to their effects on the distribution of income. A "progressive" tax takes a bigger fraction of the pre-tax income of higher income people, and thus moves the distribution of after tax income toward greater equality. A "proportional" tax takes the same fraction from everyone, and leaves the distribution of income unchanged. A "regressive" tax takes a bigger fraction of the income of lower income people, and thus increases income inequality (see Box 1).

Box 1: Regressive Taxes

As an example of a regressive tax, consider a sales tax on all goods. Since poorer people typically spend a larger fraction of their income than rich people, they will end up paying a larger fraction of their income in taxes. For example, if the government institutes a 10 percent sales tax on all goods, and a family earning $10,000 a year spends all of its income, then that family pays 10 percent of its income, or $1,000, in taxes. A family earning $100,000 a year is less likely to spend all of that income, which means that it is less likely that they will pay 10 percent of their income in taxes. A sales tax on luxuries, on the other hand—for example, a tax on 60-foot yachts, Tiffany diamonds, or Rolls Royce Silver Shadows—would probably be progressive, since it would only tax people who could afford the luxuries.

The issue of progressivity and regressivity is important because questions of *fairness* are important. While almost nobody likes to pay taxes, most people think that the tax burden should be shared in a fair way. Most think too that progressive tax systems are more fair since they require a larger proportional contribution from wealthier families whose ability to pay is greater.

Historical Background

What about the U.S. tax system? Is it progressive? An important recent study found that between 1966-80 the overall U.S. tax system—including state and local taxes as well as federal taxes—was either slightly progressive or slightly regressive, depending on certain assumptions.[12] The study found that state and local taxes were basically regressive throughout, in large part because of their reliance on sales taxes. By contrast, the federal tax system was slightly progressive throughout, but *its progressivity steadily declined*. Because of this change at the federal level, the tax system as a whole also became less progressive. As Table 3 shows, the total tax burden for the poorest tenth of the population increased by 50 percent over this period, while the burden for the next poorest 10 percent increased by 25 percent. For the wealthiest tenth of the population, on the other hand, the tax burden declined by 8 percent.

Why did the federal tax system become less progressive? Three major developments contributed to the shift.

Table 3: Effective Tax Rates by Population Group, 1966 and 1980

Population Group	1966	1980
Poorest Tenth	7.8	11.7
Second Tenth	10.2	12.8
Third	13.5	13.6
Fourth	15.1	14.8
Fifth	15.9	15.9
Sixth	16.1	16.3
Seventh	16.2	16.6
Eighth	16.6	17.8
Ninth	16.7	18.4
Richest Tenth	21.1	19.4
Richest one percent	****	18.9

Source: Joseph A. Pechman, **Who Paid the Taxes, 1966-1985**, Tables 4-12, 5-4 (using the most progressive assumptions about tax incidence).

First, throughout the postwar period, but with increasing speed after the mid-1960s, the payroll taxes that support social insurance programs increased as a share of total federal revenues (see Figure 2). Payroll taxes are regressive (see Box 2), and because they are regressive, increasing the share of federal revenue that comes from payroll taxes reduced the progressivity of the tax system.

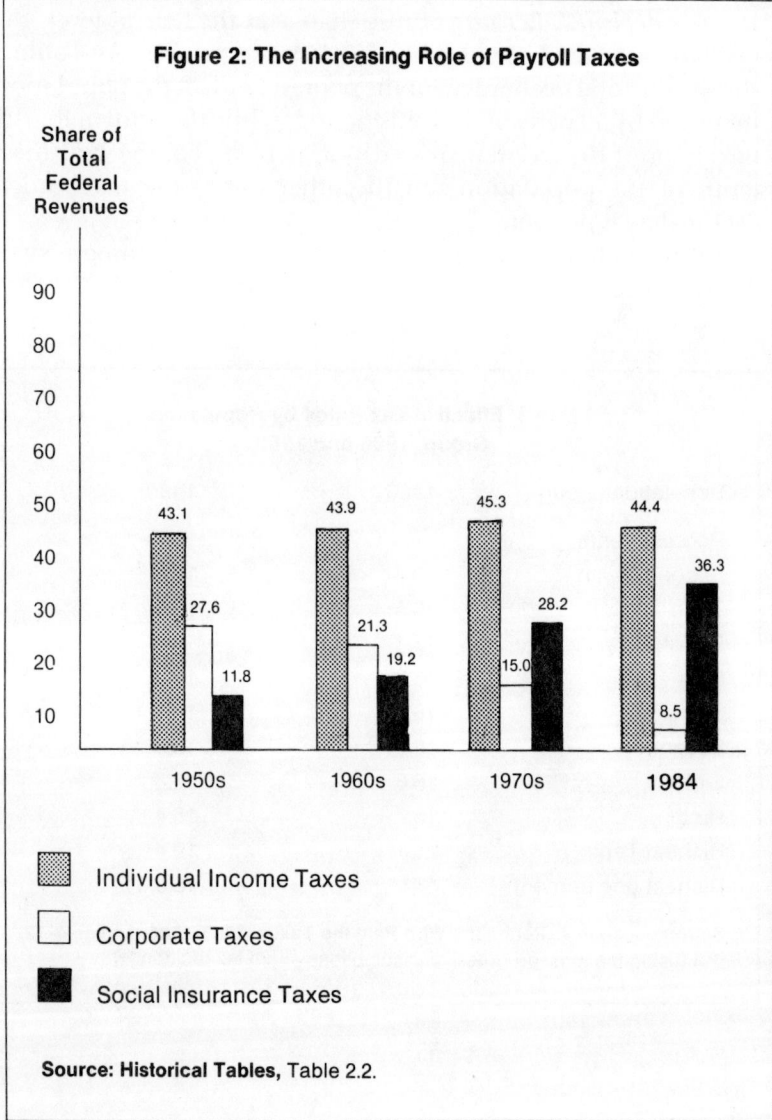

Figure 2: The Increasing Role of Payroll Taxes

Source: Historical Tables, Table 2.2.

> **Box 2: Payroll Taxes**
>
> Why are payroll taxes regressive? As their name suggests, payroll taxes are limited to wage and salary income—the chief source of income for ordinary Americans—and leave untouched the income from interest, dividends, or appreciated investments that figure prominently in the income of wealthy Americans. Moreover, they are "capped" at a certain wage and salary level, meaning that income earned beyond that level is not taxed at all. And over the income that is taxed, the rate is constant. In 1985, for example, Social Security payroll taxes claimed just over 7 percent of all wage and salary income up to nearly $40,000. So, if a worker earned $10,000, she paid about $700. Someone who earned $200,000 paid $2,800—7 percent on the first $40,000, nothing after that. For the person earning $10,000 the tax rate is 7 percent; for the person earning $200,000, it is only 1.4 percent of total income. In 1985, the poorest 10 percent paid 9.4 percent of its income in payroll taxes, while the richest 10 percent paid 3.6 percent, and the richest 1 percent paid 1.4 percent.
>
> **Source:** Joseph Pechman, **Who Paid the Taxes, 1966-1985?**

A second development contributing to declining progressivity was the declining significance of corporate taxes (see Figure 2). In the 1950s corporate taxation provided an average of 27.6 percent of federal revenue each year. In the 1970s, it provided an average of just 15.0 percent—*a more than 40 percent decline.* There is some disagreement about just who pays corporate taxes, the corporations themselves or consumers. But it is generally agreed that the reductions in corporate rates reduced the tax burdens, for upper income Americans.[15]

A third source of declining progressivity is the complicated and massive system of deductions, exclusions, credits, and exemptions —the "tax expenditures" or "loopholes"—that fill the tax code. Some tax expenditures, for example the exclusion of social security from taxation, are progressive. Others, like the investment tax credit and and special treatment for capital gains from timber income, are regressive. On balance, however, tax expenditures are regressive, and their enormous expansion over the past 20 years has also contributed to the declining progressivity of the federal tax system.[14]

Americans were not unaware of these shifts in the federal tax burden. Polls taken in the late 1970s show clearly that they realized that their taxes had increased dramatically. By 1978, 80 percent of the public thought taxes were "unreasonable," and 69 percent said they had "reached the breaking point" on the amount of taxes they paid. Most people also thought the system of federal taxation had become more unfair. Again in 1978, 74 percent of the public thought that middle income people were paying too much in taxes, while 76 percent thought high income families, and 72 percent thought large business corporations, were paying too little. Despite the much publicized "tax revolt" of the late 1970s, these beliefs did not lead the public to demand a *reduction* of taxes. It did stiffen public resistance to further tax *hikes*, however, and created strong majority support for progressive tax reform. That was not the kind of reform the public got under the Reagan administration.[15]

2 The Reagan Budget

For a generation after World War II, despite many recessions along the way, the U.S. enjoyed an unprecedented period of sustained economic growth, increasing productivity, and rising living standards. This period ended dramatically with the 1973-75 recession, the deepest economic crisis since the Great Depression of the 1930s. The Great Recession of the 1970s ushered in an era of dismal economic performance in the U.S. Growth, profits, and wages all fell dramatically, and unemployment climbed to postwar highs. The recession also highlighted dramatic changes of the structure of the international economy—and the position of the U.S. within it—that would be underscored throughout the rest of the decade. Most generally, these changes included the emergence of many Third World economies as powerful international economic actors, the decline in the U.S. competitive position, and the increasing integration of the U.S. into the world economy, with a particular deepening of U.S. relations with the Third World.

This conjunction of declining domestic economic performance and increasing integration in a competitive global economy had enormous political consequences in the U.S. The pressures it induced divided American elites, and bitter disputes raged throughout the decade over the appropriate direction of trade and monetary policy, and the conduct of relations between the U.S. and its major allies. Despite many continuing differences, however, by the end of the decade these pressures also led elite opinion to converge on three main points of action. Each had important budgetary implications.

First, there was broad elite consensus on the need for a major military buildup. This consensus grew out of the recognition that, especially in a period of growing international competition, advancing the global economic and political interests that had come to be identified as U.S. "national" interests required additional reliance on military force. Those interests could not be reliably protected by such "regional surrogates" of the U.S. as the Shah of Iran or Nicaragua's Anastasio Somoza. Nor could they be protected by international institutions not controlled by the U.S. Instead, there was growing support for a more "unilateral" approach in foreign policy—that is, an approach less reliant on the international institutions that the U.S. had helped establish at the close of World War II, and less cooperative than the sorts of strategies some U.S. figures (including Jimmy Carter) had sought to promote among the major industrial powers. Such a strategy required both sharp increases in the level of military spending and a blunt assault on the "Vietnam syndrome," or the diminished willingness of U.S. citizens to support the use of violence in U.S. dealings with Third World countries.

Second, virtually all members of the business community favored sharp further reductions in their effective tax rates. There were different rationales offered for tax reform. Some argued that general reductions were necessary to attract investment. Others claimed, more plausibly, that differences among the effective rates of taxation in different industries distorted the investment process. What nearly all U.S. business agreed on, however, was that increasing international competition made it more difficult to "pass along" taxes to consumers, and that tax cuts would generally strengthen sagging profit margins.[16]

Third, while there were sharp disagreements in the business community on the *kind* of economic program required to respond to international competition, virtually all U.S. business agreed that any program should include income losses for American workers. Suggestions about how these losses might be secured took many forms, but one area of business consensus was the virtue of cuts in social spending.

From the point of view of political and business elites, such cuts were desirable for at least two reasons. First, if there were increases in military spending *and* tax cuts (the first two points of the new consensus) then social spending cuts would help to relieve the resulting pressures on the federal budget. Second, eliminating important income supports for lower income workers would increase their dependence on the labor market. It would thus increase the "disciplining" effects of that market—that is, the tendency for high unemployment to bring wages down—and dovetail with the "tight money" policy the Federal Reserve began enforcing midway through the Carter administration. That policy, as a member of the Reagan Treasury Department later put it, aimed at increasing unemployment by "collapsing the economy."[17] As Reagan budget director David Stockman explained, a long period of high unemployment was seen as "part of the cure, not the problem" of U.S. economic difficulties.[18]

Pressures to implement these shifts in military, tax, and social spending policies were already evident during the Carter administration. A proposal for increasing the progressivity of federal taxes turned into a major business-loophole bonanza in 1978. Unemployment insurance and public service jobs programs were scaled back, and important cuts in social spending were announced in 1980.[19] In the last two years of his administration, Carter initiated major increases in the military budget.[20] And after 1978, he also presided over the initial "collapsing" of the U.S. economy.

Carter's policies, however, were never identical to Ronald Reagan's, and while commitments to increased military spending, cutbacks in social programs, and regressive revisions of the tax system have served as common premises of policy debate for several years now, those commitments reached a qualitatively different level under the current administration. The result has been a qualitative change in the shape of the federal budget.

1 Outlays: The Days of Spend and Spend

When he was running for President in 1980, Ronald Reagan promised to "get the government off the backs of the people" and to end the days of "tax and tax, spend and spend." Presidential campaign promises often depart sharply from subsequent performance. But even by conventional standards of American political debate, the gap between the rhetoric of spending reductions and actual performance during Reagan's term has been startling. By virtually any reasonable measure, the federal government has grown larger and at a faster pace since Ronald Reagan was elected president. In real terms, the government is spending more money than ever. It is also spending a bigger fraction of GNP than ever before. Even the real *rate* of increase in government spending was higher in Reagan's first term than it was during the Carter administration. Far from a slowdown of "spend and spend," federal spending has accelerated.[21]

What has changed under the Reagan administration is the *composition* of the federal budget, the shares taken by different categories and programs.

1.1 Social Spending

During the Reagan years, spending on non-military programs has been cut significantly below the levels of spending projected under pre-Reagan laws and policies. Overall, the Congressional Budget Office (CBO) estimates that policy changes since 1981 reduced spending on non-military programs by $176 billion between 1982 and 1985.

Progams directed toward low income Americans were especially hard hit. Only one tenth of the federal budget in 1980, they were victims of one third of the budget cuts enacted between 1981 and 1983.[22] As a result, the group of low income programs that we considered in Section One (see Table 2) fell from 9.3 percent of the budget in 1981 to 8.8 percent in 1985.[23] Table 4 summarizes the cuts in low income programs; as it indicates, the Administration proposed much deeper cuts than those that were enacted.

Because the low income programs were relatively small to begin with, cutting them has produced only limited budgetary savings. Because the beneficiaries of low income programs have few resources of their own, however, these cuts are enormously important to them.[24] For example:

* Benefits for most of the 20 million Americans who receive Food Stamps have been reduced. Nearly 70 percent of the savings came from people living below the poverty line.

* Some 440,000 low-income working families (virtually all headed by women) lost AFDC benefits. Several hundred

thousand more had benefits reduced. Since eligibility for Medicaid is linked to eligibility for AFDC, several hundred thousand children from low income families have also been cut from the Medicaid program. Nearly a third of all children living in poverty receive no Medicaid benefits.

* As a result of cuts in low income housing programs, an estimated 300,000 more families now live in substandard housing.

* Funding for employment and training programs was cut by more than half, dropping from $9 billion to less than $4 billion. These cuts came at a time when both the rate and average duration of unemployment in the U.S. hit record highs.

* Taken together, the budget cuts have pushed more than two million people below the poverty line.

But budget cuts have not been restricted to programs that are targeted to low income families. Unemployment insurance cover-

Table 4: Spending Reductions in 1985 as a Result of 1981-84 Policy Changes

Program	Reduction Proposed (%)	Reduction Enacted (%)
AFDC	-28.6	-14.3
Food Stamps	-51.7	-13.8
Child Nutrition	-46.0	-28.0
Low Income Energy Assistance	-37.5	-8.3
Housing Assistance	-19.5	-11.4
Medicaid	-15.7	-2.8

Source: Bawden and Palmer, "Social Policy: Challenging the Welfare State," Table 6.1.

age, for example, also fell off drastically. During the 1973-75 recession, unemployment insurance coverage was as high as 81 percent, and in the 1977 recovery, 60 percent of the unemployed received benefits. By October 1985, however, only 26.8 percent of the unemployed were covered, the lowest rate of coverage in the history of the program.[25]

The story with Social Security and Medicare was somewhat different. While combined spending on those programs in 1985 was $10 billion less than it would have been under pre-Reagan policies, their share of the budget increased slightly over the 1981-85 period, as did their share of GNP. Part of the continued rise in spending for these programs is attributable to the very high rate of inflation for health care costs (esp. for hospitalization), and the continued aging of the population. But it also reflects the greater strength of the constituencies for these programs that we noted earlier. These relative strengths are evident in the fact that, in percentage terms, both the proposed and enacted cuts in Social Security and in Medicare were less than for the low income programs. For Social Security and Medicare, Reagan proposed an 11.6 percent cut below projected spending levels; Congress approved cuts of 5.6 percent. For low income programs, Reagan proposed a cut of more than 25 percent; Congress approved cuts of about 10 percent.[26]

Finally, in noting the increased outlays for insurance programs, it is important to note as well that additional revenues were raised specifically for these programs. While there were cuts in rates for personal and corporate taxes in 1981, Social Security taxes increased in 1981, 1982, and 1985. And Medicare beneficiaries have been hit with increased premiums, co-payments, and deductibles.

1.2 Military

Developments in the military budget contrast sharply with those in the social programs. Between 1981 and 1985, the military budget grew by nearly 30 percent in real terms. This is the largest sustained peacetime buildup in U.S. history, and it represents a *qualitative departure* from the relatively flat peacetime spending levels of 1955-1980 (see Figure 3). Real spending in 1985 was 27 percent higher than the post-1950 peacetime average, and more than 15 percent above the pre-Reagan peacetime high.

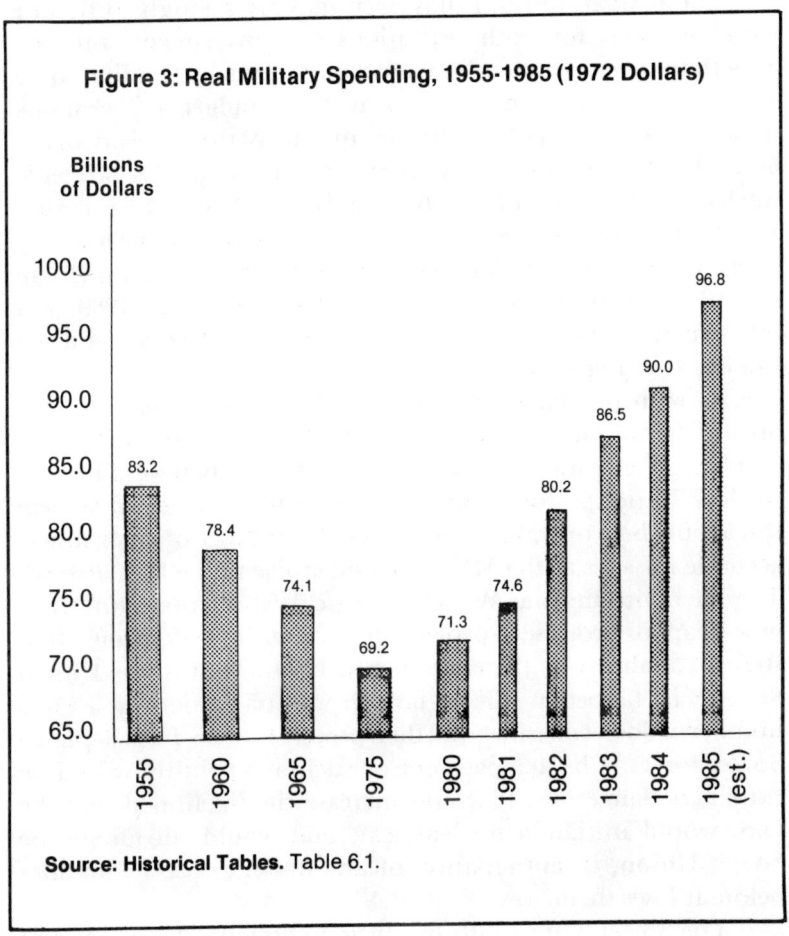

Figure 3: Real Military Spending, 1955-1985 (1972 Dollars)

Source: **Historical Tables.** Table 6.1.

In considering the aims of this buildup and in assessing its long-term budgetary consequences, it is useful to divide the military budget into two components: *operations* and *investment*. The operations component is used largely to pay military personnel and to operate and maintain existing forces. The investment component includes funds for new weapons (MX missiles, Trident submarines, B-1 bombers, Bradley fighting vehicles, F-16s, M-1 tanks), for research and development (on Star Wars, the Midgetman missile, the stealth bomber), and for military construction (for example, of bases in Honduras).

The Reagan buildup has been massive enough to permit large increases for both operations and investment. But the growth in investment has been especially dramatic, leading some analysts to describe the Reagan military budget as "weapons driven" (see Figure 4). Roughly one quarter of this investment has been devoted to the "modernization" of America's strategic nuclear forces—for building B-1 bombers, MX and D-5 missiles, and Trident submarines. The other three quarters of the military investment has gone for general purpose forces, including a huge naval buildup aimed at producing a 600 ship navy by 1989, and other such big-ticket items as F-16 fighters, M-1 tanks, and the Bradley fighting vehicle.

As with previous increases in U.S. military spending, the bulk of the current buildup is said to be directed against the Soviet Threat. Once again, however, this is difficult to believe. The U.S. nuclear buildup, for example, is creating considerable *new* threats in the world, for it increases the number of such super-accurate missiles as the MX, D-5, and cruise in the U.S. arsenal. Together with the Star Wars "strategic defense" program, these new weapons promise to provide the U.S. with a very strong "first strike" capability by the early to mid-1990s. That is, the United States will be better able to launch an attack, destroy a large number of Soviet missiles, and then protect the U.S. from depleted Soviet forces. The achievement of such a capability would be extremely dangerous. It would increase the likelihood that the U.S. would initiate a nuclear war, and would encourage the Soviet Union, in anticipation of an attack, to use its missiles before it loses them.

The Soviet Threat also has little to do with the buildup of conventional arms. To the contrary, that buildup seems largely directed toward enhancing U.S. capacities to project force into the Third World. As military analysts Barry Posen and Stephen Van Evera observe, "a significant portion of the American defense effort is now allocated to forces best suited for Vietnam-style or Dominican Republic-style interventions in Third World countries." They emphasize as well that:

> ...the Reagan administration plans to add even more, with new carriers, new "forcible-entry" amphibious assault ships, and new airlift. The administration also indicates a revived interest in intervention by rejecting a

The Reagan Budget

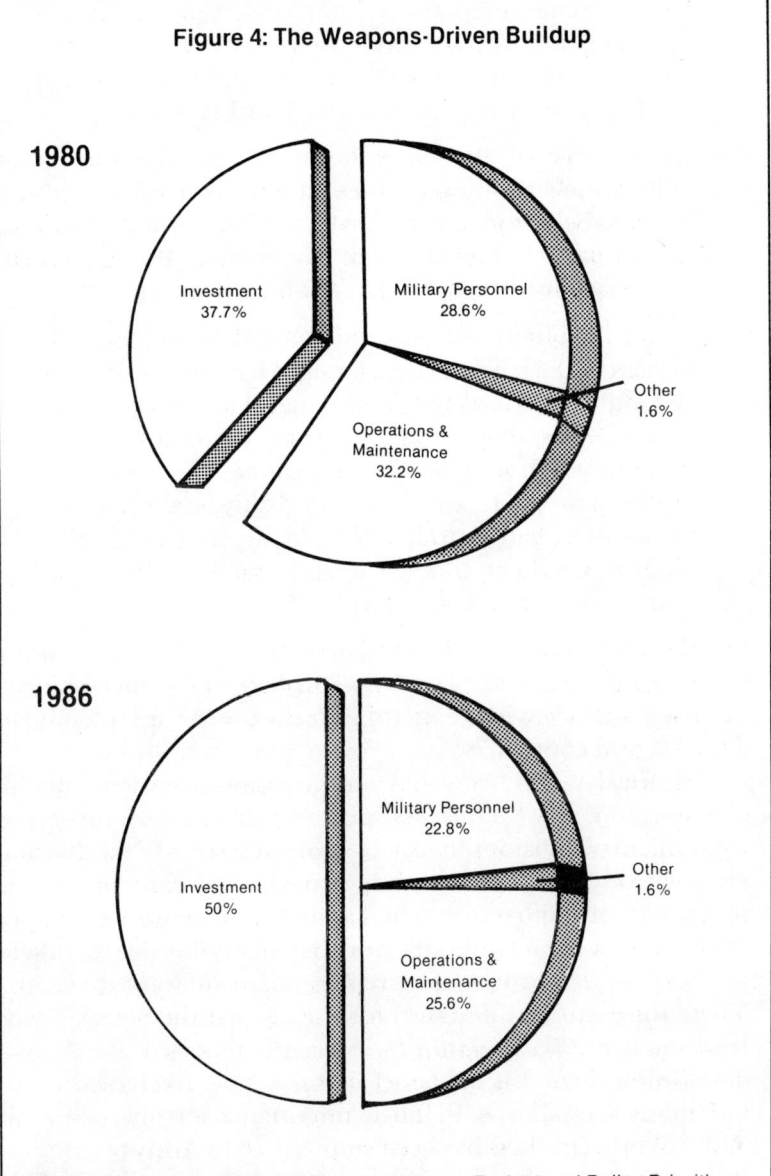

Source: The Defense Budget Project, Center on Budget and Policy Priorities, **The FY 1986 Defense Budget,** p. 54.

"one-and-a-half" war strategy, instead suggesting the United States prepare to fight on several fronts simultaneously. This represents a shift toward intervention, since more "half wars" in addition to Korea would probably be fought in the Third World.[27]

The centerpiece of the Navy buildup, for example, is the Administration's addition of three aircraft carrier battle groups. These, it has been said, are needed to do battle with the Soviets at their major bases in Murmansk or Vladivostok. But as respected defense specialist William W. Kaufmann points out:

> As for the offensive against Murmansk or Vladivostok, the extent that such an attack might have merit, it could be conducted as readily by long-range, land-based aircraft as by carriers, despite the propensity to argue that only naval forces should be allowed to attack naval targets... Furthermore, if the attack depended only on the power of three carrier battle groups, the odds are rather high that all three would be disabled or sunk and that a large part of the Soviet fleet would survive.[28]

On the other hand, as hawkish military analyst (and former Carter Undersecretary of Defense) Robert W. Komer observes: "Carriers still serve many useful purposes. They are splendid for Third World conflict."[29]

Similarly, the Army has recently converted two infantry divisions to a new "light" design, and plans to form three more light infantry divisions (two active, one reserve). These divisions are relatively small and lightly armed; they contain a larger percentage of combat troops and a smaller percentage of support troops than standard divisions; and they are deployable worldwide as much as three times as fast as standard infantry divisions.[36] These forces are not designed for use against the Soviet Union. Instead, as the *Washington Post* recently reported, the Army is developing them "in the belief that the most likely war on the horizon is a small one."[31] Their importance for lower-intensity Third World conflicts has been emphasized in Army briefings on the rationale for the light forces, which have focused on Third World scenarios for their use.[32] And the 1985-1986 *American Defense Annual* notes that their development signals the Army's aim to "accommodate the special requirements of Third World contingencies in the conventional force structure."[33]

The development of additional forces for Third World intervention also illuminates the Reagan administration's strategy in developing new nuclear weapons.[34] Members of the Reagan administration see an *unbreakable link* between U.S. advantages in strategic nuclear forces and U.S. willingness to use its conventional forces. In their view, the strategic nuclear forces serve as the final guarantee of the capacity of the United States to use non-nuclear force in local conflicts, and are thus a key instrument in the ordinary conduct of foreign policy. This view, we should note, is not unique to the Reagan administration. In his last Annual Report as Carter's Secretary of Defense, for example, Harold Brown also underscored this role of the strategic forces by stating that, "with them, our other forces become meaningful instruments of military and political power."[35] But members of the current administration have been unusually clear about the connection between nuclear and conventional weapons. Eugene Rostow, co-founder of the hawkish Committee on the Present Danger and former head of the Arms Control and Disarmament Agency, has declared that "the true moral (sic) of Vietnam" is that "the deterioration of our nuclear advantage led to the erosion of our position, and profoundly affected the final stages of the conflict."[36] For Rostow, the nuclear weapons provide a "persuasive influence in all aspects of diplomacy and of conventional war."[37] Alexander Haig, too, has emphasized that the strategic balance "casts a shadow over every significant geopolitical decision. It affects on a day-to-day basis the conduct of American diplomacy. It influences the management of international crises and the terms on which they are resolved." [38]

This view about the political importance of strategic forces underscores the "deadly connection" between the Reagan administration's buildup of nuclear forces and its pursuit of broadly unilateralist and interventionist military policies. We will return to this connection below in our discussion of intervention in Central America. Now, however, we turn to the *budgetary* consequences of the weapons-driven buildup.

Like other investment decisions, a decision to invest in a weapon commits resources for the future and therefore imposes limits on future choices. This point cannot be overemphasized in a discussion of military budgeting. On average, only 14 percent of the money authorized by Congress for weapons procurement is actually paid out in the first year after the Congressional decision, and less than half is spent in the first two years. If the government decides in 1986 to spend $15 billion on a new missile, for example, in 1988 $7.5 billion will likely remain unspent. But much of the unspent billions will *already be obligated* by contracts signed in 1986. Because such contracts are hard to break, the unspent money cannot just be shifted to other uses. In the jargon, it is "locked in."

Decisions made in the past few years have sharply curtailed the range of military programs that can be cut now, or in the future. As more and more of the military budget has gone to weapons acquisition, more and more of the military budget has become "uncontrollable." This has obvious consequences for deficit reduction proposals. In effect it requires that spending cuts come either from non-weapons parts of the military budget that are more controllable, or from spending for programs that benefit poor and middle class Americans.

1.3 Interest on the Debt

Despite its unprecedented growth, however, the military budget has *not* been the fastest growing line in the federal budget: interest payments on the federal debt have grown much faster. In the first four years of Reagan's presidency, federal deficits increased from $78 billion to $210 billion, and the federal debt nearly doubled, jumping from $1 trillion to almost $2 trillion. As a result, interest payments grew by nearly 60 percent, and climbed from 10.1 percent of the budget in 1981 to 13.6 percent in 1985.[39] The need to meet interest payments places one more constraint on federal spending. But it is also likely to increase the degree of inequality in the United States.[40]

To see why, consider the fact that the United States is a very unequal society, and that its most striking inequalities occur in the ownership of financial assets—stocks, bonds, money invested in money market accounts, IRAs, checking accounts, etc. As Table 5 indicates, in 1983 the wealthiest 10 percent of American families (families earning over $50,000) held 72 percent of the stock and 70 percent of the bonds; the wealthiest 2 percent held 50 percent of the stock and 39 percent of the bonds. Evidence suggests that the ownership of Treasury bonds, bills, and notes, like the ownership of financial assets generally, is also very unequally distributed. This means that the interest payments on the debt are similarly unequally distributed, so that wealthier Americans

Table 5: Ownership of Financial Assets, 1983

Asset Type	Percent Held by Families at Upper Income Levels	
	Top 10 percent	Top 2 percent
Checking Account	41	23
Savings Account	26	8
Money Market Account	40	15
Certificate of Deposit	33	15
IRA	48	17
Savings Bonds	26	12
Stocks	72	50
Bonds	70	39

Source: Robert B. Avery, et. al., "Survery of Consumer Finances, 1983," **Federal Reserve Bulletin,** vol. 70 (September 1984)

appear to be the primary beneficiaries of Treasury interest payments.

Who finally pays this interest? That depends on how the deficit problem is addressed. Under the most likely deficit-reduction scenarios—whether the Gramm-Rudman Balanced Budget Amendment (see Box 3) remains in effect or is found unconstitutional—the main burden of deficit reduction will be placed on spending cuts, with perhaps some role for tax increases. Since interest payments cannot be cut, the spending cuts will fall at least in part on social programs. Resources now used for social programs will instead go to pay interest on the debt. But social programs primarily benefit the poor and middle classes, while interest payments disproportionately benefit the wealthy. For example, 93 percent of the Food Stamps go to the poorest 40 percent of the population. By contrast, more than half of federal interest payments go to the wealthiest 20 percent of the population. Thus, as the portion of the budget devoted to social programs drops and the portion devoted to interest payments increases, the government will be raising the level of inequality.

If simple tax increases (without progressive tax reform) are used to cover the deficit, the result will also likely be greater inequality, since the percentage of taxes paid by high income

> **Box 3: Gramm-Rudman and Deficit Reduction**
>
> Signed by President Reagan in December of 1985, Gramm—Rudman—officially the "Balanced Budget and Emergency Deficit Control Act"—introduces several fundamental changes in the budget process. The most important change is a new process for meeting deficit targets. Gramm-Rudman sets annual limits on the deficit (starting with $171.9 billion for 1986, and dropping to $0 in 1991). If the tax and spending bills passed by Congress do not stay under these ceilings, then there will be automatic cuts from the levels of spending approved by Congress.
>
> Nearly half the cuts will come from military programs, the rest from non-military. Several non-military programs will be exempt from the automatic cuts, including: Aid to Families with Dependent Children, Child Nutrition, Food Stamps, interest payments, Medicaid, Social Security, Supplemental Food Program for Women, Infants, and Children, Supplemental Security Income, and Veteran's pensions and compensation. Five health programs, the largest being Medicare, can be cut by no more than one percent in 1986 and two percent thereafter.
>
> Keep in mind that Gramm-Rudman sets deficit targets, and that the automatic cuts go into effect only if Congress fails to meet them. It does not dictate the way to meet the targets. Congress could, for example, pass a stiff minimum tax on corporations and individuals or considerable reductions in the military budget. Or they could eliminate virtually all domestic spending. Under Gramm-Rudman **something must give**: either there has to be a tax increase, or a drop in the military budget, or cuts in programs that benefit low and middle income Americans, or the elimination of Gramm-Rudman. While it remains on the books, however, Gramm-Rudman will highlight the very grave costs for most Americans of the Reagan era regressive tax cuts and weapons-driven military buildup.

Americans is less than the percentage of interest payments that they receive. In 1983, for example, the wealthiest 20 percent of the population received 53.1 percent of the interest payments; in 1985 that same 20 percent paid 48.2 percent of the taxes. Given the present tax system, an increase in taxes to cover the interest payments will therefore effectively transfer resources to wealthier Americans.

There are, of course, other less probable deficit reduction strategies. Congress could pass a special law imposing a deficit reduction tax on corporations and on Americans earning more

The Reagan Budget 33

than $100,000 a year. Or they could repudiate some of the debt. Or the Federal Reserve could dramatically increase the money supply, and effectively allow the government to pay off the debt with inflated dollars. Each of these policies might be widely beneficial, but none of them is very likely, since each would be strongly opposed by holders of the debt.

What is most likely, therefore, is that the sharp increases in interest payments will reinforce the increased inequality produced by other Reagan spending initiatives. This movement towards greater inequality has also been accelerated by Reagan decisions in tax policy.

2 Tax Cuts: Feeding the Hogs

While the composition of the budget has changed, the days of spend and spend continue. What about the days of tax and tax? Are Americans paying lower taxes? It depends on who you are. Many people in the U.S. now have a much heavier tax burden than they did in 1981; others have a much lighter one. The changes in burdens have been dramatically regressive. In 1980, the average two parent, family of four living at the poverty line paid $460 in taxes, about 5.5 percent of their $8,400 income. By 1985 a family of four at the poverty line paid $1,147, or 10.4 percent of their $11,000 income.[41] Those at the very top of the U.S. income pyramid, making more than $200,000 a year, enjoyed spectacular declines in their tax burden. For families in between (see Table 6), the changes in tax burden moved consistently with income class, as the tax system accelerated down the same regressive path it had taken over the previous 15 years.

Several tax initiatives contributed to these shifts. The "supply-side," across-the-board tax cuts of 1981 played a role, since they provided much larger reductions for higher income Americans than lower income Americans. The reason for this is simply that higher income Americans pay more taxes, and the more you pay, the more you gain from across-the-board cuts. David Stockman commented at the time that the supply-side incentives were really just a "Trojan horse to bring down the top rate"—a way to decrease the tax rates for higher income Americans. They succeeded in doing just that.[42]

And while the proportional across-the-board cuts were formally neutral, other changes in the tax system were not. Over

Table 6: Estimated Changes in 1984 Tax Bills as a Result of 1981 Tax Cuts, Inflation, and Increased Social Security Taxes

Income Level (1981)	% of Taxpayers (1981)	Change in 1984 Tax Bill ($$)	Change in 1984 Tax Bill (%)
$0-10,000	34.2	+108	+24
$10,000-15,000	14.7	+126	+7
$15,000-20,000	12.1	+30	+1
$20,000-30,000	18.9	-74	-2
$30,000-50,000	15.2	-276	-4
$50,000-100,000	4.0	-953	-6
$100,000-200,000	0.7	-4,169	-14
$200,000+	0.2	-21,348	-17

Source: Robert S. MacIntyre and Dean C. Tipps, **Inequity and Decline** (Washington: Center on Budget and Policy Priorities, 1983), Figure 7.

the past four years, increases in Social Security taxes, the failure to increase the "zero bracket" (the income level at which no federal taxes need to be paid), the cut in tax rates on unearned income, the expansion of the regressive system of deductions, credits, exemptions, and exclusions, and the drop in inheritance taxes all conspired to produce the results shown in Table 6.

In addition to these shifts in taxes on individuals, the Reagan administration nearly succeeded in eliminating taxes on corporations by providing a "Christmas tree" of tax benefits to corporations in 1981. Stockman said of the negotiations during the decoration of this tree that "The hogs were really feeding. The greed level, the level of opportunism, just got out of control."[43] Nevada Senator and long-time Reagan friend Paul Laxalt explained the lobbying techniques that were used: "[o]ne of the greatest things that was done was to go through the lists of big contributors and get them to lean on swing people. If a big contributor calls and says 'Go along with this,' it has a big effect."[44] By 1983, corporate taxes produced only 6.2 percent of all federal tax revenue. Changes in the tax laws in 1982 recouped some of this revenue. But the corporate tax continues to generate only an estimated 9 percent of federal revenue, one third of the average for the 1950s, and less than half the average for the 1960s.

The Reagan Budget 35

After the passage of the 1981 tax cuts, several hundred lobbyists held a party to celebrate the "End of the Corporate Tax."[45] A recent study by Citizens for Tax Justice shows why they were celebrating.[46] The study considers the taxes paid by 275 major corporations with pretax profits in excess of $400 billion between 1981 and 1984. Of the 275 companies, 129 paid either no taxes at all or received tax rebates in at least one of the years between 1981 and 1984, and 50 of the 275 paid a total of nothing or less over the four year period as a whole. This group of 50 includes five of the largest dozen military contractors—General Dynamics, General Electric, Lockheed, Boeing, and Grumman. Three other of the top dozen military contractors (McDonnell-Douglas, Martin Marietta, and Westinghouse) paid less than 1 percent of their profits in taxes. Altogether the top dozen enjoyed an effective federal income tax rate of only 6.3 percent between 1981 and 1984, about half the tax rate of the average American family.

3 The Bottom Line: Inequality and the Politics of Deficits

Apart from the arms buildup, the two most striking consequences of the Reagan budgets are growing inequality and enormous deficits.

Inequality and poverty have increased dramatically:

* In 1984 the gap between upper and lower income families was greater than in any year since the Census Bureau began collecting this information in 1947. The poorest 40 percent of families (families earning less than $21,700 a year) received 15.7 percent of national income, their smallest share since 1947. The middle 20 percent received 17 percent, their smallest share since 1947. The top 40 percent received 67.3 percent of national income, their largest share since 1947.[47]

* Some 33 million Americans—one in every seven—lived below the poverty line in 1984, an increase of 4.4 million over 1980 and an increase of 9 million over 1978. Nearly one quarter of all children below the age of six now live in poverty, and more than half of all black children under six—51.1 percent—live in poverty.[48]

* As we have seen, tax cuts for upper income Americans, and benefit losses for lower income Americans have both contributed to growing inequality. A recent Congressional Budget Office (CBO) report estimated the effects of changes in 1981 and 1982 for household incomes during 1983-85. Combining tax and benefit changes, the CBO found that households earning less than $10,000 experienced a net loss of $367 a year. By contrast, households with incomes over $80,000 gained more than $8,000.[49]

Deficits have increased even more dramatically. There is considerable debate about the *economic* consequences of those deficits—about the extent to which federal deficits are the source of high interest rates, record trade deficits, continued high levels of unemployment, massive loss of manufacturing jobs, the devastation of American agriculture, and the deflationary pressure on foreign economies that continue to mark the Reagan economic "miracle." But whatever the outcome of the debate on the economics of deficits, three aspects of the political causes and consequences of the deficit situation are already clear and commonly acknowledged.

First, as we have already indicated, the deficits have produced a massive expansion of interest payments which will likely contribute to growing inequality.

Second, the deficits have their roots in the combination of increased military spending and the regressive shifts in the tax system initiated in 1981. The Congressional Budget Office estimates that some 60 percent of the $210 billion 1985 deficit resulted from the tax and military spending policies of the Reagan administration. If the policies in effect when Reagan came into office in 1981 had not been changed, 1985 tax revenues would have been $111 billion greater, military spending $35 billion lower, interest payments $21 billion lower, and nondefense spending $38 billion higher. With no cuts in domestic programs, the 1985 deficit would have been about $80 billion, just over a third of its actual level.[50]

Third, it is now widely acknowledged that the growth in the deficit was not an accidental byproduct of Administration policies, but the result of a deliberate policy choice. As Senator Patrick Moynihan (who voted for the Reagan tax plan in 1981) has put it, the Administration made a "deliberate decision to create deficits for strategic, political purposes."[51] Or as former Reagan Assistant Treasury Secretary Paul Craig Roberts has explained: the Administration was "determined to use the deficit to focus congressional attention on the budget."[52] The plan was to permit high deficits, in the expectation that these deficits would result in intense pressure on Congress to reduce the programs of the Great Society and the New Deal. As the current debate about deficit reduction and the consequences of Gramm-Rudman (see Box 3) sharply underscores, the budget deficit is already having these effects. Just why it is may be clarified by considering the alternative deficit reduction strategies.

Tax increases would be one obvious strategy. But it is always difficult to raise taxes in the United States in peacetime. There has been no peacetime increase in individual income taxes since a very small hike in the late 1930s.[53] The 1982 corporate tax hike, which took back a piece of the 1981 give-a-way to corporations, was the first peacetime increase of any sort since 1939. Moreover, the tax changes introduced in the Economic Recovery and Tax Act of 1981 will be particularly hard to change, since they index brackets to inflation, thus forcing tax increases to be made explicitly. Significant increases in corporate taxes above their pre-Reagan levels also seem unlikely, since the same pressures that led business to demand reductions continue. These pressures against tax increases are reflected in the fact that all the major current proposals to reform the tax system are "revenue neutral." None of them raises the total level of taxes paid to the federal government.

Holding tax revenues constant, deficit reduction becomes a "zero-sum game." Gains for one program come at the expense of others. As we have seen, the Administration has been quite successful thus far in shielding military spending from cuts, and building in long term obstacles to reducing the military budget. As we have also seen, rising interest payments are another constraint. In combination, and without tax increases, military and interest payment commitments impose long term pressures on social spending that will continue beyond Reagan's second term. The combination of tax cuts, a weapons-driven military buildup, and politically-manipulated deficits have already altered the terms of political debate in the United States. They will comprise the political legacy of this administration.

Of course the strategy of initiating large deficits to force Congress to cut domestic programs could backfire. In the debate over the 1986 budget, the level of new authorizations for the military was frozen at 1985 levels. And the broader debate on the budget, deficit reduction, and the consequences of Gramm-Rudman has focused public attention on the massive military buildup of Reagan's first term. Where that debate will go, and whether it will produce yet further increases for the military, or marginal reductions in the military budget, or rather a more serious and fundamental reconsideration of present military policy, remains an open political question. This brings us to the topic of Central America.

3 Central America: A Budgetary Perspective

1 The Policy Framework: Low-Intensity Warfare/High Intensity Symbolism

What are the connections between the budget and Central America? In order to address this question, we need to begin by seeing U.S. policy in the region in terms of the interests and ambitions of current policy makers (see Box 4 on Central America).

First, from the very first days of the Reagan presidency, Central America has served as the high-intensity symbol of the more aggressive U.S. foreign policy that has marked the Reagan years. Members of the Administration have repeatedly emphasized the close ties between its broader aim of restoring U.S. power to pre-Vietnam levels and its policies in that region. U.S. policies toward Central America are seen by Administration figures as critical to establishing the "credibility" of its aims and power around the world:

* Commenting on El Salvador during the 1980 campaign, one Reagan advisor said that: "El Salvador itself doesn't really matter. We have to establish credibility because we're in very serious trouble."[54]

* In 1981 U.N. Ambassador Jeane Kirkpatrick insisted that: Central America is the most important place in the world for the United States today."[55]

> **Box 4: Central America: The Basics**
>
> **Guatemala**
>
> Population: 7.1 million
> Area: 42,000 square miles (about the size of Kentucky)
> Economy: coffee, bananas, cotton
> Illiteracy: 60 percent
> Income per person: U.S. $1,198
>
> **El Salvador**
>
> Population: 4.75 million
> Area: 8,236 square miles (size of Massachusetts)
> Economy: coffee exports, U.S. assistance
> Illiteracy: 50+ percent
> Income per person: U.S. $680
>
> **Honduras**
>
> Population: 3.7 million
> Area: 43,000 square miles (about the same as Louisiana)
> Economy: banana and coffee exports
> Illiteracy: 60 percent
> Income per person: U.S. $640
>
> **Nicaragua**
>
> Population: 2.7 million
> Area: 57,000 square miles (about the size of North Carolina)
> Economy: coffee, cotton, sugar, timber exports
> Illiteracy: 60-70 percent before 1979 revolution
> Income per person: U.S. $897
>
> **Costa Rica**
>
> Population: 2.5 million
> Area: 20,000 square miles (smaller than Arkansas)
> Economy: depends on coffee, banana, sugar exports
> Illiteracy: less than 10 percent
> Income per person: U.S. $1,520
>
> **Source:** Walter Lafeber, **Inevitable Revolutions** (New York: W. W. Norton, 1983), pp. 8-11.

* Echoing the same theme, Henry Kissinger, the Chairman of the President's National Bipartisan Commission on Central America, observed that: "if we cannot manage in Central America, it will be impossible to convince threatened nations in the Persian Gulf and in other places that we know how to manage the global equilibrium."[56]

Central America: A Budgetary Perspective 41

* And Reagan himself underscored the *high-intensity symbolism* of Central America in a speech to a joint session of Congress:

> If Central America were to fall, what would the consequences be for our position in Asia and Europe and for alliances such as NATO? If the United States cannot respond to a threat near our own borders, why should Europeans or Asians believe we are seriously concerned about threats to them?... If we cannot defend ourselves there, we cannot expect to prevail elsewhere. Our credibility would collapse, our alliances would crumble and the safety of our homeland would be put at jeopardy.[57]

Second, and as part of the resurgence of interventionism already noted, there has recently been renewed interest among military and foreign policy analysts in improving strategies for supporting insurgency and counter-insurgency efforts around the world. This interest has focused on the potential of *low-intensity warfare*.[58] In his 1986 Annual Report, for example, Secretary of Defense Weinberger asserted that "low-level conflict will likely remain the most immediate threat to free world security for the rest of this century."[59] There is little consensus about just what makes a conflict low-intensity. But analysts generally agree that the aim in a low-intensity conflict is for U.S. interests to prevail without committing large numbers of U.S. ground troops. To avoid such commitment, the U.S. government must be prepared to engage in long-term programs of funding, support, and advice for insurgency and counter-insurgency forces, to pursue economic and psychological warfare, as well as covert action, and if need be, to deploy smaller numbers of U.S. troops specially trained and organized for Third World conflicts.

Third, the U.S. has pursued and continues to pursue a low-intensity strategy in Central America—building bases, running constant ground and naval exercises, pursuing covert operations, psychological warfare, and economic blockades, and providing money, weapons, and military training to insurgency and counter-insurgency forces. From a political point of view, the central consequence of this low-intensity strategy is that the direct and perceived costs of the policy remain relatively low for the U.S. From the standpoint of assessing more general U.S. ambitions, however, it is already clear that Central America is a *testing ground* for new U.S. interventionist capabilities and strategies.[60]

These three factors—high-intensity symbolism, low-intensity warfare, and Central America's status as a testing ground—provide the framework for our analysis of the costs of current U.S. policy in the region.

2 U.S. Policy in Central America: "No Free Lunch"

As just noted, an important political advantage of low-intensity warfare is that it keeps the direct costs of an aggressive military policy relatively low and out of the public eye. But the costs of U.S. policy in Central America and the Caribbean are *not negligible*, and they are growing. For 1985, we estimate those costs at $9.5 billion, nearly eight times the $1.2 billion officially acknowledged by the Reagan administration.

Estimating these costs is a complicated matter, in part because the Reagan administration has an interest in representing its current strategy as a low-budget operation. It recognizes that in the current budgetary environment, with so much attention concentrated on the need for cuts in spending, the more costly a policy is, the closer the scrutiny it will receive.[61]

Despite the complexities and the partly speculative nature of cost estimates, however, such assessments are worth making. They are made for other regions that are of interest to the U.S.—for example, for Western Europe and East Asia—and making them for Central America and the Caribbean is important if we are to understand the costs of asserting U.S. power in the Third World and the domestic costs of maintaining the military apparatus required to assert such power.[62]

2.1 "Security" Assistance

The most widely discussed cost of U.S. policy is "security" assistance. In 1985 the U.S. spent more than $1.4 billion on all forms of foreign assistance (including economic and security assistance) for Central America. This represents a more than 20-fold real increase over the $68 million spent in 1978.[63] Table 7 shows how the money was allocated by country, and Table 8 lists U.S. "assistance" programs in the region. Some of these programs are classified as economic assistance, some as security assistance, but the classifications themselves are controversial.

Table 7: Assistance to Central America, 1985

Country	Level of Assistance ($ millions, estimated)
Costa Rica	218.8
El Salvador	562.2
Guatemala	89.9
Honduras	282.1
Panama	84.6
Belize	22.0
Regional Programs	174.1
	1433.7

Source: Stephen R. Harper and Larry Q. Nowels, "Central America and U.S. Foreign Assistance: Issues for Congress," U.S. Library of Congress, Congressional Research Service, July 24, 1985, Issue Brief 84075, Appendix.

Table 8: Foreign Assistance Programs

Economic Assistance	Development Aid
	Peace Corps
	Subsidized Food Sales
	Humanitarian Food Aid
	Investment insurance for U.S. investors
Security Assistance	International Military Education and Training
	Military Assistance Program
	Foreign Military Sales Guarantees
	Economic Support Fund

Source: Jonathan E. Sanford, "U.S. Foreign Assistance to Central America," U.S. Library of Congress, Congressional Research Service, March 2, 1984, Report No. 84-34 F.

President Reagan has repeatedly insisted that U.S. aid to the region is primarily economic and not security assistance. Addressing a joint session of Congress in April 1983, for example, he claimed that "77 cents out of every dollar we will spend in the area this year goes for food, fertilizers, and other essentials for economic growth and development."[64] This common, but very misleading, Administration claim is based on a mischaracterization of the Economic Support Fund (ESF) program. Administered by the State Department, ESF is now by far the largest U.S. assistance program for the region, and is the source of more than half of all U.S. assistance.[65] Because the program is so big, counting it as an economic program permits the President to count "77 cents out of every dollar" as economic aid.

We will classify ESF as security assistance, however, and for several reasons. First, while it is true that ESF provides dollars to help governments finance imports, it provides those dollars only to countries of major foreign policy significance to the United States. The largest recipients of the ESF assistance are Israel and Egypt. Many countries with far more serious financial and development problems receive nothing at all. Second, ESF assistance permits recipients to devote other resources to military ends. The $285 million that the Administration provided El Salvador in 1985, for example, helped that government finance imports from the United States. But, like "humanitarian" aid to the contras, this "economic" assistance also enabled the government of El Salvador to use other resources to pursue its military goals—including its savage air war against its own population.[66]

Third, while our judgment differs from the President's, it is not that controversial. The Administration's own foreign aid budget lists ESF, together with military aid, under the heading of "security assistance." And a recent report by the Congressional Research Service on U.S. assistance to Central America points out that a number of experts agree with this classification. They argue that "the ESF in Central America is *basically a security/military program* undertaken to prop up the existing regimes and the elites who support them."[67]

Counting the ESF program as a security/military program, then, $998 million—or nearly 70 percent of U.S. assistance to Central America—now goes for security/military assistance. This represents a significant shift from 1980, when 26 percent of U.S. aid was for security, while 74 percent was economic.

2.2 Maintaining Presence

The costs of the security assistance program represents only the surface of a much deeper and more costly military effort in the region. The U.S. maintains a large and growing military presence in Central America and the Caribbean, and any complete estimate must include the costs of maintaining this presence and threat. These costs have several components:

Military Exercises: In 1981, the U.S. held two military exercises in the region. In 1982, there were five exercises, in 1983 there were 10. By 1984, the number of U.S. military exercises had grown to 20. They have continued on a routine and continuous basis throughout 1985. Some of the operations are small. Lightning II, for example, was a one-day exercise on April 13, 1984 involving 120 U.S. Army troops and 170 Honduran Special Forces. Others are huge. Ocean Venture 84, a two week joint Army, Navy, Air Force, and Marine Corps operation, involved 30,000 U.S. troops, an aircraft carrier, 350 ships, and 250 planes. Big Pine II lasted for six months and at its peak involved 5,500 U.S. troops in Honduras and more than 16,000 troops on ships and planes. These military exercises often overlap one another. In mid-November 1984, there were six simultaneous exercises, five of which were directed against Nicaragua.[68]

Military Construction: There has been considerable military construction in the region, particularly in Honduras. There are now eight to ten airbases that can handle large transports, and two to three bases (Palmerola, San Pedro Sula, and perhaps Goloson) that are capable of handling high performance fighter planes.[69]

Forces: The U.S. also has forces stationed in the region. More than 9,000 troops are in Panama (including the 193rd Infantry Brigade), some 1,700 are regularly in Honduras, 1,500 in Bermuda, 2,500 at Guantanamo in Cuba, 3,500 in Puerto Rico, and 70 in El Salvador.[70]

A complete accounting of the region must include the costs of all the naval and ground exercises, of the military construction, and of the forces based in the region. This would likely run to more than $3 billion a year—$2.5 billion for the forces, $500 million for the exercises, and some $100 million for the construction.[71] Together with the security assistance, this pushes the total costs of U.S. policy in the region to nearly $4 billion.

2.3 No Force Without Forces

Leaving things there, however, would also seriously underestimate the costs, since the costs of *exercises* are still only the tip of U.S. involvement. In order to exercise forces and be prepared to use them in a direct intervention, the forces themselves must be available. A complete accounting of annual costs must therefore also include the costs of *buying* and *supporting* at least some of the forces that are exercised in the region and at least some that would be used in the event of a military intervention.

The assessment here proceeds in two steps. The first is to estimate the costs of buying and supporting different sorts of the major military forces—Army and Marine ground divisions, air wings, and carrier battle groups. We estimate that, on average, it costs $2.5 billion per year for a ground division and $3.5 billion for a carrier battle group.[72]

The second step is to assess how many of such units are assigned to a particular region. Assigning forces to the region is complicated because Central America and the Caribbean, unlike Western Europe and East Asia, do not have a large complement of forces officially designated or "programmed" for them. Determining the the actual force assignments for the region thus requires looking beyond the "formal" or "programmed" force commitments, and assessing what portion of other forces should be included in an accounting of regional military costs. Inevitably, such assessing requires making judgments, and for this reason *any* realistic assessment will be "soft" and subject to controversy. But there is no way around this problem. While any realistic assessment will be controversial because it involves making judgments, the failure to make such judgments would require us to accept an assessment that is obviously distorted.

As an example of the problem, consider ground forces. There is a U.S. Southern Command, headquartered in Panama, which has responsibility for Central and South America. But there are not many forces assigned to it and those that are assigned only partially account for the scope of the U.S. commitment in the region. The ground forces that are regularly exercised in the region and that would be used if there were an invasion, for example, are not permanently assigned to this Command. They come instead from the so-called U.S. Readiness Command, and are available for use in the Persian Gulf and for rapid deployment missions in other regions, as well as in Central America.[73]

Should some of the costs of these other forces be counted in the costs of current U.S policy in Central America and the Caribbean? Yes, we think they should. The Army's annual statement for 1986 asserts that "regional conflicts in the Middle East, Asia, or Latin America" are "more probable" than a general war, emphasizing the importance of Central America in current military planning.[74] Since 1983 the Army has also been devoting considerable resources to the development of the light infantry divisions that we discussed earlier, forces which are designed for use primarily in low-intensity conflicts in the Third World (see Box 5).

Central America has been prominent in discussions of the "low-intensity threats" that prompted the development of these light divisions. A recent study of the light infantry initiative asserts that "In internal Pentagon briefings on the light divisions, the Army has...emphasized their possible use in Central

---

Box 5: What's Behind the Mules?

One of the new light infantry divisions is the 10th Mountain Division, stationed at Fort Drum, New York. General John Wickham, Army Chief of Staff and father of the light divisions, has recently instructed the 10th to begin training in mule handling. Although he is an Army man, Wickham may have been inspired by the experience of the Marines during the 1927-1933 war against Sandino in Nicaragua. According to a 1929 **Marine Corps Gazette** article, mules are "the most suitable of any animal obtainable in Nicaragua." A 1965 article in the **Gazette** on the "lessons" that the war against Sandino held for fighting in Vietnam and the Dominican Republic emphasized the virtues of using mules in mounted patrols in order to conserve "the energy of trail weary Marines for the more important business of fighting."

Sources: "Professional Notes," in **Marine Corps Gazette,** vol. 14, no. 4 (December 1929), p. 298; "Guerrilla Lessons From Nicaragua," in **Marine Corps Gazette,** vol. 49 (June 1965), pp. 32-40. We would like to thank David Brooks for providing the material on the mules which initially came to our attention in an article in NACLA's **Report on the Americas,** vol. 19, no. 6 (November-December 1985) p.3

America." This same study quotes a Pentagon official as saying that "Central America is pretty high up on the list." Another "ranking Pentagon official" is cited as offering the following explanation of the initiative: "The Army is trying to increase its budget share, and Central America and the non-Western world is where the action is in terms of money and prestige."[75] Some of the costs of these ground divisions should be charged to the policy in Central America and the Caribbean.

We make similar calculations and judgments about naval forces. Given the intensity of Navy operations in the region, and the magnitude of the recent buildup of the Navy, it seems reasonable to assign the costs of some naval forces to the region.

Taking all of this into account—the attention to Central America that is demonstrated by the Administration's high-intensity symbolism, the constant military exercises, the military construction, the emphasis on the region in discussions of the new light divisions, and the forces that would be needed for direct intervention—we charge two ground divisions ($2.5 billion per division) and one carrier battle group ($3.5 billion) to Central America and the Caribbean. These costs (which include the $3.2 billion already noted for forces stationed in the region and for exercises and military construction) add $8.5 billion each year to the $1 billion of security assistance. Taking all the costs together, we come out at roughly $9.5 billion spent annually on current U.S. military/security policies toward Central America and the Caribbean.

It bears emphasis again that this estimate is soft. Others disagree with the forces we charge to the region. Some put the costs slightly lower, at $7 billion; others put them much higher, at $19 billion.[76] Reasonable analysts can disagree about where in this range the costs should be fixed. But *any* reasonable estimate will be higher than the Administration's $1.2 billion, because any reasonable estimate will include the high costs of building, maintaining, and replacing the military apparatus—the capital goods—required for carrying out current policies.

2.4 Balance Sheets

Our review of the direct costs of U.S. policies in the region highlights again the issue of spending priorities. While $9.5 billion dollars is only 1 percent of the federal budget, it is a considerable amount in the current budgetary environment. If spent otherwise in 1985, the $9.5 billion would have been sufficient to restore the funds cut from several important social programs during the first three years of the Reagan presidency. Table 9 shows how $9.5 billion could have been used in 1985 to restore programs to where they would have been without the Reagan cuts.

Table 9: Three Balance Sheets

Program	Reagan Spending Reduction (in billions 1985 $)
Aid to Families with Dependent Children	1.4
Food Stamps	2.0
Child Nutrition Programs	1.4
Vocational Education	0.1
Unemployment Insurance (two thirds)	3.4
Medicaid	0.7
Social Services Block Grant	0.8
	9.8
Or,	
Social Security	9.2
Low Income Energy Assistance	0.2
	9.4
Or,	
Medicare	5.4
Public Service Employment (½)	2.4
Guaranteed Student Loans	1.6
	9.4

Source: D. Lee Bawden and John L. Palmer, "Social Policy: Challenging the Welfare State."

3 What Next?: The Costs of Invasion

The $9.5 billion estimate of annual costs is *not* an estimate of the costs of a U.S. invasion in the region. Such an invasion cannot be ruled out, and the repeated military failures of the contra in Nicaragua will continue to encourage the Administration to invade (see Box 6). The exercises and construction serve in part as training and preparation for direct U.S. military intervention. According to a June 1985 report in the *New York Times* "the military is prepared for contingencies," and "the buildup of the Southern Command [the division of the military with "responsibility" for Central America]...is now largely complete and... adequate to carry out any likely emergency in the region."[77]

What would an invasion cost the U.S.? It depends of course on the level and scope of local resistance. On all accounts that resistance would be intense in either El Salvador or Nicaragua. One conservative accounting of the costs to the United States of an invasion of Nicaragua, which makes the very improbable assumption that an invasion of Nicaragua would not lead to a regional war, maintains that an invasion would cost $16 billion over a five year period. Some 2,000-5,000 Americans would be killed, 9,000-19,000 would be wounded, and a one-and-a-half division U.S. occupational force would remain in Nicaragua for at least five years. According to these same analysts, the costs to the Nicaraguans themselves "are likely to be very much higher."[78]

Box 6: Never Say "Never"

"We have never interfered in the internal government of a country and have no intention of doing so, never have had any thought of the kind."

—Ronald Reagan

U.S. Interventions in Nicaragua

1853	1899 (twice)
1854	1910 (twice)
1857 (twice)	1912-1925
1867	1926
1894	1926-1933
1896	1981-present
1898	

Source: U.S. Library of Congresss Foreign Affairs Division, "Background Information on the Use of U.S. Armed Forces in Foreign Countries: 1975 Revision," 94th Congress, 1st Session (Washington, D.C.: U.S. Goverment Printing Office, 1975), pp.58-66.

4 Broadening the Debate: The Costs of Intervention

In assessing the costs of U.S. policy in Central America we have restricted our attention to the direct costs of that policy. But, as we underscored at the beginning of Part III, Central America is the high-intensity symbol and testing ground for a much broader interventionist policy. If the Reagan administration is "successful" in Central America, that success will encourage them elsewhere. As a result, there is no simple way to separate the direct costs of U.S. policy in Central America from the broader costs of a generally interventionist foreign policy. Our assessment of the direct costs of the policy in Central America has shown that it requires a considerable and expensive military apparatus. The broader interventionist policy requires an even greater one.

We should begin by emphasizing again that assessments of the cost of that apparatus are both complicated and speculative, and are rarely pursued by military analysts. Those who do pursue them, however, agree that the interventionary forces include at least some of the aircraft carrier task forces (five to nine of the 15 in Reagan administration plans), six to ten of the 17 active Army divisions (especially the lighter and more mobile divisions), two to three Marine divisions, the Special Operations Forces, as well as some airlift, sealift, and amphibious ships. This is a massive commitment of resources.[79]

But the costs of intervention go beyond the costs of conventional weapons. As we indicated earlier, there is a close and deadly connection between the development of strategic nuclear forces and conventional interventionary forces. Anyone concerned about intervention should be also be concerned about the nuclear buildup, and anyone concerned about the nuclear buildup needs to consider the degree to which that buildup is driven by interventionist policies. The question here is what (if any) nuclear forces the U.S. needs for defense against the Soviet Union, and which serve to enhance our interventionary capabilities? Like many others, we see no justification, based on considerations of defending the U.S., for the MX missile, B-1 bomber, Trident submarine, Trident II missile, or, more generally, for more than a submarine-based deterrent.

Several analysts have proposed military budgets based on the principles of defending the U.S. and not interfering in the affairs of other states. Once again, estimates are difficult, but one such budget, proposed by the Security Project of the World Policy Institute, estimates that $125 billion could be saved from 1989 military spending by reducing the strategic nuclear forces to a submarine force (with nearly 6000 warheads), reducing the number of ground divisions from 20 to 12, eliminating eight aircraft carriers and 51 amphibious ships, reducing the Navy from 650 to 400 ships, and eliminating three of 44 air wings.[80] Some analysts committed to the same principles argue that smaller reductions are appropriate, others propose even larger reductions.[81] Whatever their differences in matters of detail, however, all such proposals indicate that considerable resources are currently devoted to forces keyed to intervention, and therefore show as well that current policies in Central America and the Caribbean are not only another "dirty little war" waged by the U.S. against much smaller and less powerful nations, but the cutting edge and leading example of a massive military commitment.

4 Conclusion:
Drawing the Line in Central America

We began this pamphlet by asserting that the domestic initiatives of the Reagan administration are related to its foreign policy. By analyzing changes in the composition and financing of the U.S. budget, we hope to have shown the truth of that assertion. The massive buildup of an already enormous military establishment, and the aggressive actions abroad that that establishment permits, are paid for with taxpayer money. The cutbacks in domestic spending that permit the buildup come at the expense of the American people, and increase inequality among them. Budgets are filled with numbers, but they are "not merely matters of arithmetic." They tell political stories, and the political story the U.S. budget tells again and again is that U.S. commitments to an aggressive military policy abroad come at the expense of justice at home.

In recent months, the pressure of $200 billion deficits and the requirements of Gramm-Rudman have again focused attention on the enormous size of the military budget, and encouraged wide-ranging criticisms of the shape and direction of military spending. The best publicized criticisms have focused on military contract scandals—on the purchase of $9,000 hammers and $600 toilet seats. More serious criticisms have been directed against the duplication of weapons systems, the role of inter-service rivalries in encouraging wasteful procurement policies, the emphasis on unnecessarily complex and expensive "high-tech" weapons, and excessive spending on new weapons at the cost of deemphasizing the readiness of existing forces.

But while each of these criticisms is important, and each has some merit, none gets to the heart of the matter. Eliminating all the waste, fraud, and abuse now reflected in "defense" outlays still leaves an enormous military budget. And that budget is enormous because of the foreign policy role that the U.S. government has assigned to the military since the 1950s, and that the Reagan administration has forcefully reasserted. As Eugene McCarthy observed of the military budget: "It's not the fat that ought to worry us, it's the lean."

Military force is a central instrument in the conduct of America's foreign policy. High military budgets do not only reflect that policy; they are a necessary precondition to its pursuit. There is thus no reasonable way to separate a discussion of the military budget from a discussion of what that budget is for. To get at the lean of military spending requires reexamining the goals of U.S. foreign policy, and for criticism of the military budget to be effective, it must be joined with criticism of the uses to which military force is put.

These uses are various, but as we have emphasized, the links between different parts of the military budget are tighter than is commonly assumed. The Reagan administration has promoted a more interventionist foreign policy, and has sought the military forces required for it. Its strategists see the nuclear buildup as necessary to the effective use of a variety of new conventional forces for fighting small and low-intensity wars in the Third World. And its development of those conventional forces and the pursuit of the interventionist policies that they permit, can in turn be expected to heighten tensions between the superpowers. In so doing, they also increase the likelihood of nuclear war. There is a "deadly connection" between the different parts of the military buildup.

We have seen too—from the actions as well as the declarations of the Reagan administration—that Central America is the cutting edge of the Administration's interventionist policy. It is a high-intensity symbol of U.S. resolve to intervene around the world, and a testing ground both of the willingness of people in the United States to tolerate such acts and of the military capabilities that will make them possible.

Conclusion

And we have seen that the direct costs to U.S. taxpayers of current U.S. policies in Central America are substantial—$9.5 billion each year—and vastly larger than the costs acknowledged to by the Administration. When these direct costs are added to the economic costs of other interventionist forces, the yearly total rises over $100 billion. This expanded measure of costs indicates just how high the stakes of U.S. policy in Central America really are.

At this point we come full circle, back to the domestic tradeoffs that current U.S. foreign policies imply. Annual savings of $100 billion are not trivial, and especially at a time of social spending cutbacks and continued domestic economic turmoil, alternative and more constructive uses for this money can easily be imagined. More than enough to eliminate poverty in this country and to restore social programs to their pre-Reagan levels, the funds might be used to rebuild U.S. cities, educate its children, retrain its workers, or clean up its polluted environment. If the U.S. wanted, some could even be used abroad—to feed the millions of children who die each year of starvation, or to provide medical supplies to those who live.

Finally, considering such alternatives reminds us of something we have known all along—that we have both the capacity and the obligation to judge the morality of present policies. In Washington these days there is much talk about "hard choices" on deficit reduction and as it happens we are writing these words on January 15, 1986, the day that the first of the automatic spending cuts of Gramm-Rudman were announced. Whether Gramm-Rudman survives or not, more cuts will be coming soon, and more "hard choices" will be made. But a consideration of recent trends in the U.S. budget, including the increased costs of U.S. aggression in Central America, shows that the "hard choices" urged by the Reagan administration are really false choices. They answer the wrong question. Budgets do not only tell political stories. They *are* those stories, a record of the decisions a society has made about how it wishes to order itself and its relation to the rest of the world. And the real question raised by any budget is not "how much do things cost" but, "are these the right things to be spending money on?" What should really be at issue in present budget controversies is not how much more the U.S. should spend to export violence abroad, or how much less generous it should be toward its own people, but *whether* present policy commitments should be pursued at all. Central America is a good place to begin asking that question.

As it happens, today is not only the first day of Gramm-Rudman, it is also the anniversary of the birth of Martin Luther King. More than any other American leader in the past generation, King recognized the domestic consequences of American foreign policy. This is what led him in 1967 to "break silence" and publicly oppose the Vietnam War. But King recognized as well the consequences of that policy for those against whom it was directed. Listen to what he said about the U.S. war against Vietnam:

> Somehow this madness must cease. We must stop now. I speak as a child of God and brother to the suffering poor of Vietnam. I speak for those whose land is being laid waste, whose homes are being destroyed, whose culture is being subverted. I speak for the poor of America who are paying the double price of smashed hopes at home and death and corruption in Vietnam. I speak as a citizen of the world, for the world as it stands aghast at the path we have taken. I speak as an American to the leaders of my own nation. The great initiative in this war is ours. The initiative to stop it must be ours.

Today the war has moved to Central America. The power to stop it remains at home.

FOOTNOTES

1. Office of Management and Budget, *Historical Tables: Budget of the United States Government, Fiscal Year 1986* (Washington, D.C.: U.S. Government Printing Office, 1985), Table 3.1.
2. *Ibid.*
3. See Seymour Melman, *Pentagon Capitalism: The Political Economy of War* (New York: McGraw-Hill, 1970), and *The Permanent War Economy* (New York: Simon and Schuster, 1974); and Gordon Adams, *The Iron Triangle: The Politics of Defense Contracting* (New York: Council of Economic Priorities, 1981).
4. The discussion of "force without war" is based on Barry Blechman and Stephen Kaplan, *Force Without War* (Washington, D.C.: The Brookings Institution, 1978). More than 60 of the 215 cases—or one every 6 months—were in Latin America (p. 20).
5. George Kennan, "A Modest Proposal," *New York Review of Books*, 16 July 1981, pp. 14-16.
6. Blechman and Kaplan, *Force Without War*, p. 36.
7. On the bomber and missile gaps, see Fred Kaplan, *Wizards of Armageddon* (New York: Simon and Schuster, 1983); on the "window of vulnerability" and other rationales for the Reagan buildup, see Jeff McMahan, *Reagan and the World: Imperial Policy in the New Cold War* (New York: Monthly Review Press, 1985), esp. chaps. 2 and 3.
8. Stanley Hoffmann, Samuel P. Huntington, Ernest R. May, Richard N. Neustadt, and Thomas C. Schelling, "Vietnam Reappraised," *International Security*, vol. 6, no. 1 (Summer 1981), p. 14.
9. All the numbers on the size of social programs come from *Historical Tables*, Tables 11.3., 13.3. "Basic" programs include Social Security, Medicare, and the low income programs listed in note 10.
10. For the purposes of the discussion here, we confine our attention to the following low income programs: Medicaid, housing assistance (budget function 604), food and nutrition assistance (budget function 605), and public assistance and related programs (budget function 609 plus veteran's non-service pensions). We thus leave out compensatory education, student financial assistance grants, Head Start, and a variety of other low-income programs. This simplifies the discussion but does not affect the substantive points.
11. William Greider, *The Education of David Stockman and Other Americans* (New York: Dutton, 1982), p. 60.
12. On the shifting tax burden, see Joseph A. Pechman, *Who Paid the Taxes, 1966-1985* (Washington, D.C.: The Brookings Institution, 1985), chapter 5.
13. *Ibid.*, Table A-4.
14. See John F. Witte, *The Politics and Development of the Federal Income Tax* (Madison: The University of Wisconsin Press, 1985), section

IV; and U.S. Congress, Joint Committee on Taxation, "Estimates of Federal Tax Expenditures for Fiscal Years 1984-1989," 9 November 1984 (Washington, D.C.: U.S. Government Printing Office, 1984).

15. On public opinion on taxes, see Everett Carll Ladd, Jr. (with Marilyn Potter, Linda Basilick, Sally Daniels, and Dana Suszkiw), "The Polls: Taxing and Spending," *Public Opinion Quarterly* 43 (Spring 1979), p. 127; and Witte, *Politics and Development*, p. 342.

16. On business efforts to change the tax code, see Robert S. McIntyre and Dean C. Tipps, *Inequity and Decline* (Washington, D.C.: Center for Budget and Policy Priorities, 1983), pp. 49-57.

17. Paul Craig Roberts, *The Supply-Side Revolution* (Cambridge, MA: Harvard University Press, 1984), pp. 223-24.

18. Cited in *ibid.*, p. 225.

19. For discussion of disputes within the American business community during this period and their political consequences, see Thomas Ferguson and Joel Rogers, "The Reagan Victory: Corporate Coalitions and the 1980 Campaign," in *The Hidden Election: Politics and Economics in the 1980 Presidential Campaign*, eds. Thomas Ferguson and Joel Rogers (New York: Pantheon, 1981), pp. 3-64; Thomas Ferguson and Joel Rogers, *Right Turn: The Decline of the Democrats and the Future of American Politics* (New York: Hill & Wang, 1986); and our discussion in *On Democracy* (New York: Penguin, 1983), chapter 4.

20. On Carter administration military programs, see Robert Komer, "What 'Decade of Neglect'?" *International Security*, vol. 10, no. 2 (Fall 1985), pp. 70-83. According to Komer, "Reagan rhetoric [during his first term] tended to obscure the fact that Reagan's program was mostly an acceleration of a buildup already begun under Carter." (p. 79)

21. *Historical Tables*, Table 6.1 (using February 1985 estimates for 1985 spending).

22. This figure is based on two studies by the Congressional Budget Office. The first, *Major Legislative Changes in Human Resource Programs Since 1981*, August 1983, p. vii, shows a $57 billion drop in low income programs for 1982-1985. The second, *The Economic and Budget Outlook: Fiscal Years 1986-1990*, February 1985, p. 153, shows a $176 billion cut in non-defense spending as a result of policies enacted since 1981.

23. *Historical Tables*, Table 11.3.

24. The material that follows comes from Center on Budget and Policy Priorities, *Smaller Slices of the Pie* (Washington, D.C.: November 1985), pp. 22-25.

25. *Ibid.*, p. 19; see also John Bickerman, *Unemployed and Unprotected: A Report on the Status of Unemployment Insurance* (Washingon, D.C.: Center on Budget and Policy Priorities, March 1985).

26. D. Lee Bawden and John L. Palmer, "Social Policy: Challenging the Welfare State," in John L. Palmer and Isabel V. Sawhill, eds., *The Reagan Record* (Cambridge, MA: Ballinger, 1984), Table 6.1.

27. Barry R. Posen and Stephen W. Van Evera, "Reagan Administration Defense Policy: Departure From Containment," in *Eagle Defiant: United States Foreign Policy in the 1980s*, eds. Kenneth A. Oye, Robert J. Lieber, Donald Rothchild (Boston: Little, Brown, 1983), pp. 86-7.

28. William W. Kaufmann, *The 1986 Defense Budget* (Washington, D.C.: The Brookings Institution, 1985), p. 35.

29. Robert W. Komer, *Maritime Strategy or Coalition Defense?* (Cambridge, MA: Abt Books, 1984), p. 74.

30. For description of the forces see Caspar W. Weinberger, *Annual Report to Congress, Fiscal Year 1986*, in U.S. Congress, House Committee on Appropriations, Subcommittee on the Department of Defense, 99th Congress, 1st Session, *Department of Defense Appropriations for 1986* (Washington, D.C.: U.S. Government Printing Office, March 1985), vol. 1, pp. 370, 417-18, 506-9.

31. "Army Forming Light Divisions," *Washington Post*, 26 December 1985.

32. Michael R. Gordon, "The Charge of the Light Infantry—Army Plans Forces for Third World Conflicts," *National Journal*, 19 May 1984, pp. 968-972.

33. Robert H. Kupperman and William J. Taylor, Jr., "Special Supplement: Low-Intensity Conflict, the Strategic Challenge," in *American Defense Annual: 1985-1986*, eds. George E. Hudson and Joseph Kruzel (Lexington: Heath, 1985), p. 213.

34. For discussion of the connections between intervention and nuclear forces see Joseph Gerson, ed., *The Deadly Connection: Nuclear War and U.S. Intervention* (Philadelphia: New Society, 1986); Randall Forsberg, "Confining the Military to Defense as a Route to Disarmament," *World Policy Journal*, vol. 1, no. 2 (Winter 1984), pp. 285-318; Robert Borosage, "What Drives the Arms Buildup," *END: Journal of European Nuclear Disarmament*, Feb.-March 1984; Michael Klare, "The Deadly Connection: Intervention and Nuclear War," *Freeze Focus*, June 1984; "The Conventional Weapons Fallacy," *The Nation*, 9 April 1983; "Leaping the Firebreak," *The Progressive*, Sept. 1983. (The articles by Borosage and Klare are available as Institute for Policy Studies Reprints.)

35. Harold Brown, *Annual Report to Congress, Fiscal Year 1981* (Washington, D.C.: U.S. Government Printing Office, 1980), p. 5.

36. Eugene Rostow, *SALT II—A Soft Bargain, A Hard Sell: An Assessment of SALT in Historical Perspective* (Washington, D.C.: Committee on the Present Danger, 1978), p. 13, cited in Jerry Sanders, *Empire At Bay: Containment Strategies and American Politics at the Crossroads* (New York: World Policy Institute, 1983), p. 6.

37. "The Case Against SALT II," *Commentary*, February 1979, p. 23.

38. Cited in Richard Feinberg, *The Intemperate Zone: The Third World Challenge to U.S. Foreign Policy*, (New York: W.W. Norton, 1983), p. 220.

39. *Historical Tables*, Tables 1.1, 3.1.

40. The following discussion of the distributional consequences of the increasing role of interest payments in the federal budget draws on unpublished data made available to us by the Urban Institute; and Thomas Michl, "Contractionary and Reactionary," unpublished paper. We would like to thank Gerald Epstein and Juliet Schor for helpful discussions of this issue.

41. *Smaller Slices of the Pie*, p. 33.

42. Greider, *Education of David Stockman*, p. 49.

43. *Ibid.*, p. 58.

44. Cited in McIntyre and Tipps, *Inequity and Decline*, pp. 50-51.

45. Citizens for Tax Justice, "Corporate Taxpayers and Corporate Freeloaders" (Washington, D.C., August 1985), p. 11.

46. *Ibid.*, pp. 1-6 for the material in this paragraph.

47. *Smaller Slices of the Pie*, p. 3 (based on the most recent Census Bureau studies on income distribution).

48. *Ibid.*, p. 7.

49. Congressional Budget Office, *The Combined Effects of Major Changes in Federal Taxes and Spending Programs Since 1981*, Staff Memorandum, April 1984, Table 5.

50. Congressional Budget Office, *The Economic and Budget Outlook: Fiscal Years 1986-1990*, Part 1, Appendix D, Table D-2.

51. "Reagan's Inflate the Deficit Game," *New York Times*, 21 July 1985.

52. Roberts, *Supply-Side Revolution*, p. 173.

53. For discussion, see Witte, *Politics and Development of the Federal Income Tax*, chapter 12.

54. Cited in William LeoGrande, "A Splendid Little War," *International Security*, vol. 6, no. 1 (Summer 1981), p. 27.

55. Cited in Walter Lafeber, *Inevitable Revolutions* (New York: Norton, 1983), p. 4.

56. *New York Times*, 19 July 1983.

57. *New York Times*, 28 April 1983.

58. For discussion of low-intensity conflict, see Michael Klare, "The New U.S. Strategic Doctrine," *The Nation*, 28 December 1985, pp. 697, 710-16; Eliot A. Cohen, "Constraints on America's Conduct of Small Wars," *International Security*, vol. 9., no. 2 (Fall 1984), pp. 151-81; Donald R. Morelli and Michael M. Ferguson, "Low-Intensity Conflict: An Operational Perspective," *Military Review* (November 1984), pp. 2-16; Kupperman and Taylor, "Special Supplement: Low-Intensity Conflict, the Strategic Challenge."

59. Caspar Weinberger, *Annual Report to Congress, Fiscal Year 1986* (Washington, D.C.: U.S. Government Printing Office, 1985), p. 27.

60. For discussion of U.S. military actions in the region, see American Friends Service Committee, *Invasion: A Guide to the U.S. Military Presence in Central America* (Philadelphia, 1985); Caribbean

Basin Information Project, *On a Short Fuse: Militarization in Central America* (Washington, D. C., 1985).

61. For an example of such sensitivity, see the March 1985 interchange on Contra aid between Congressman Norman Dicks (D-Washington) and former Assistant Secretary of State for Inter-American Affairs Langhorne Motley in U.S. Congress, House Committee on Appropriations, Subcommittee on the Department of Defense, 99th Congress, 1st Session, *Department of Defense Appropriations for 1986* (Washington, D.C.: U.S. Government Printing Office, March 1985), vol. 2, pp. 1138-9.

62. For one method of making such estimates, see Earl C. Ravenal, *Defining Defense: The 1985 Military Budget* (Washington: Cato Institute, 1984). The Weinberger Defense Department is reluctant to attribute forces to regions, since many units are available for more than a single region. For criticism of this reluctance, see Ravenal, p. 16.

63. For 1978, see Jonathan E. Sanford, "U.S. Foreign Assistance to Central America," U.S. Library of Congress, Congressional Research Service, 2 March 1984, Report No. 84-34 F, p. 7. On current levels of assistance, see Stephen R. Harper and Larry Q. Nowels, "Central America and U.S. Foreign Assistance: Issues for Congress," U.S. Library of Congress, Congressional Research Service, 24 July 1985, Issue Brief 84075, Appendix. The money spent in 1985 includes funds appropriated in 1984 supplementals, but not obligated in 1984.

64. *New York Times*, 29 April 1983.

65. For discussion of ESF see Richard Alan White, *The Morass: United States Intervention in Central America* (New York: Harper and Row, 1984), chapter 10; and the Congressional Research Service Reports cited in footnote 62.

66. On the air war in El Salvador, see the regular reports by Americas Watch, most recently "The Continuing Terror: Seventh Supplement to the *Report on Human Rights in El Salvador*" (New York: September 1985), pp. 10-38.

67. Sanford, "U.S. Foreign Assistance to Central America," p. 9.

68. See Caribbean Basin Information Project, *On a Short Fuse*.

69. Figures based on information provided by the Central American Historical Institute. For a good general discussion of the situation in Honduras, see Phillip Shepard, "Troubled 'Allies' and Fragile Peace," *World Policy Journal*, vol. 2, no. 1 (Fall 1984), pp. 109-54.

70. The International Institute for Strategic Studies, *The Military Balance 1984/85* (London: International Institute for Strategic Studies, 1984).

71. The $2.5 billion for the forces comes from the fact that there is roughly the equivalent of a division stationed in the region, and that each division costs $2.5 billion (see next footnote). The estimates for the exercises and military construction comes from Michael Klare, "A Vietnam at Reagan's Door," *South*, June 1984. Klare's estimates are for 1984.

72. The costs per unit come from conversation with William Kaufmann. We are of course responsible for any errors in the estimate presented here. Kaufmann's unit costs are considerably below those in Ravenal's *Defining Defense*, pp. 15-6. The difference results chiefly from the fact that Ravenal distributes all budget authority across different force components and does not include reserves, while Kaufmann distributes outlays, less retirement accrual and intelligence, and does include reserves. There are many ways of estimating these costs, and not much weight should be attached to the precise numbers. The point is to get a better qualitative appreciation of the costs of a policy that relies on demonstrations of a willingness and an ability to use military force, though not necessarily on the actual use of that force.

73. *New York Times*, 4 June 1985.

74. John O. Marsh, Jr. and General John A. Wickham, *The Posture of the Army*, in U.S. Congress, House Committee on Appropriations, Subcommittee on the Department of Defense, *Department of Defense Appropriations for 1986*, vol. 2, p. 184.

75. See Michael R. Gordon, "The Charge of the Light Infantry—Army Plans Forces for Third World Conflicts," pp. 968-972.

76. For the $19 billion, see Michael Klare, "The U.S. Defense Commitment in Latin America," *The Tribune*, 19 April 1984, B-4. Another analyst suggested $6 billion for the forces in conversation.

77. *New York Times*, 4 June 1985.

78. Theodore H. Moran, "The Costs of Alternative U.S. Policies, 1984-1989," in *Central America: Anatomy of Conflict*, ed. Robert Leiken (New York: Pergamon, 1984), pp. 166-68.

79. For discussion of these costs see Feinberg, *The Intemperate Zone*, chap. 4; Randall Forsberg, "Confining the Military to Defense as a Route to Disarmament"; Barry R. Posen and Stephen W. Van Evera, "Overwhelming and Underarming," *Foreign Policy*, no. 40 (Fall 1980), pp. 99-118; Posen and Van Evera, "Reagan Administration Defense Policy"; Ravenal, *Defining Defense*; and World Policy Institute, *The Security Project: First Report* (New York, July 1984).

80. *The Security Project*, p. 59.

81. Smaller savings are indicated in Feinberg, *The Intemperate Zone*, pp. 222-3, larger savings in Ravenal, *Defining Defense*.

RESOURCES
Prepared by Joy Hackel

1. For information on the federal budget and Central America contact the institutions affiliated with Policy Alternatives for the Caribbean and Central America:

    Center for the Study of the Americas
    2288 Fulton Street #103
    Berkeley, CA 94704
    (415) 540-5006

    Central America Resource Center
    P.O. Box 2327
    Austin, TX 78768
    (512) 476-9841

    Institute-for Food and Development Policy
    1885 Mission Street
    San Francisco, CA 94103
    (415) 864-8555

    Institute for Policy Studies
    1901 Q Street, NW
    Washington DC 20009
    (202) 234-9382

    North American Congress on Latin America
    151 West 19th Street
    New York, NY 10011
    (212) 989-8890

2. For additional information on the federal budget contact:

    American Friends Service Committe
    National Action/Research on the Military Industrial Complex
    1501 Cherry Street
    Philadelphia, PA 19102
    (215) 241-7175

    Center for Budget and Policy Priorities
    The Defense Budget Project
    236 Massachusetts Ave., NE, Suite 301
    Washington DC 20002
    (202) 546-9737

    Center for Defense Information
    1500 Massachusetts Ave., NW
    Washington DC 20002
    (202) 862-0700

    Children's Defense Fund
    122 C Street, NW, Suite #400
    Washington DC 20001
    (202) 628-8787

Clergy and Laity Concerned
198 Broadway
New York, NY 10038
(212) 964-6730

Jobs With Peace
76 Summer Street
Boston, MA 02108
(617) 451-3389

National Training and Information Center
954 West Washington Blvd.
Chicago, IL 60607

3. Solidarity Networks: These networks can refer you to regional centers for further information.

Committe in Solidarity with the People of El Salvador
Box 50139
Washington DC 20004
(202) 393-3370

National Network in Solidarity with the Nicaraguan People
2025 Eye Street, NW, Suite #1117
Washington DC 20006
(202) 223-2328

Network in Solidarity with the People of Guatemala
930 F Street, NW #720
Washington DC 20004
(202) 483-0050

4. Religious Networks: The task forces listed below provide resources and listing of Protestant, Jewish, and Catholic local affiliates across the U.S.:

Inter-Religious Task Force
475 Riverside Dr., Room #633
New York, NY 10015
(212) 870-3383

New Jewish Agenda
149 Church Street, #2N
New York, NY 10007
(212) 227-5885

Religious Task Force on Central America
1747 Connecticut Ave., NW
Washington, DC 20009
(202) 387-7652

Resources

5. For additional resources on Central America, contact:

Center for International Policy
120 Maryland Ave., NE
Washington DC 20002
(202) 544-4666

Central America Historical Institute
Intercultural Center
Georgetown University
Washington DC 20057

Central America Peace Campaign
1822 R Street, NW
Washington DC 20009
(202) 232-3197

Central America Research Institute
P.O. Box 4797
Berkeley, CA 94704
(415) 843-5041

Commission on U.S. Central America Relations
1775 T Street
Washington DC 20009
(202) 332-4830

Ecumenical Program for Interamerican Communication
and Action (EPICA)
1470 Irving Street, NW
Washington DC 20010
(202) 332-0292

Honduras Information Center
1 Summer Street
Somerville, MA 02143
(617) 625-7220

National Central America Health Rights Network
853 Broadway, Suite #1105
New York, NY 10003
(212) 420-9635

National Labor Committe in Support of Democracy and Human Rights in El Salvador
15 Union Square
New York, NY 10003
(212) 242-0700

Office Of the Americas
1227 4th Street
Santa Monica, CA 90401
(213) 451-2428

Pledge of Resistance
c/o Emergency Response Network
1101 O'Farrell Street
San Francisco, CA 94109

The Resource Center
P.O. Box 4726
Albuquerque, NM 87102
(505) 266-5009

Washington Office on Latin America
110 Maryland Ave., NE
Washington DC 20002
(202) 544-8045

Women's Coalition to Stop U.S. Intervention in Central America and the Caribbean
475 Riverside Dr., Room #812
New York, NY 10115
(212) 870-2359

OTHER PACCA PUBLICATIONS

The next pamphlet in PACCA's Domestic Roots series will be:

Rules of the Game (Joshua Cohen and Joel Rogers): an analysis of the evolution and structure of the U.S. political system, particularly as it relates to the development of the Central America movement (South End Press, July 1986).

Other PACCA publications include:

Changing Course: Blueprint for Peace in Central America: an outline for U.S. policy in the region which continues to be used as a basis for "peace alternatives." (Institute for Policy Studies, Washington D.C.: $5.00. An accompanying study guide is available for 50¢.)

Transition and Development: Problems of Third World Socialism: a critical examination of the problems encountered when Third World countries attempt a socialist transformation to alleviate poverty and repression. (Monthly Review Press, NY $11.00)

Joshua Cohen is an associate professor of philosophy and political science at the Massachusetts Institute of Technology. Joel Rogers is an assistant professor of political science at Rutgers University, Newark. They are the co-authors of **On Democracy** (New York: Penguin Books, 1983).

In their perceptive analysis of the budget, Cohen and Rogers reveal the essence of the Reaganite program: enrich the wealthy, oppress the poor, and eliminate, by violence if necessary, any threat to this conception of domestic and world order. As they demonstrate, the people of Central America have been selected as the prime victims of a program that is global in intent. Their analysis exposes with great clarity the true face of the reactionary jingoism that currently shapes state policy.

—**Noam Chomsky**

Priority reading for every member of the peace movement in America.

—**Maggie Kuhn**
National Convener, Gray Panthers

Cohen and Rogers offer exactly the kind of study activists need: one that exposes the links between this government's inequitable domestic policy and its anti-democratic, interventionist foreign policy. Such a resource is crucial for movement-building today.

—**Mel King**

Here at last is an accounting of the real cost of global intervention—a cost whose burden falls heaviest upon low-income women, children, minorities, and the unemployed.

—**Barbara Ehrenreich**

This insightful document finally brings the cost of U.S. intervention **home.**

—**Charlie Clements, MD**

In the era of Gramm-Rudman...students will find **Inequity and Intervention** extremely useful in the battle to maintain the education budget.

—**Tom Swan**
President, United States Student Association

Inequity and Intervention shows how the vast sums being spent on Central American adventures are taken out of the pockets of America's workers.

—**William Winpisinger**
President, International Association of Machinists and Aerospace Workers

Inequity and Intervention is a vital tool for work with religious and grass roots constituencies.

Marjorie Tuite, O.P.
President, National Assembly of Religious Women

SOUTH END PRESS

$4.75
cover design by Mike Prokosch

International/Economics
0-89608-325-X